两个西南
Two Southwests

edited by
李森 Li Sen
龙晓滢 Long Xiaoying
Steven Schroeder 史蒂文·施罗德
王浩 Wang Hao
张晓红 Zhang Xiaohong

VIRTUAL ARTISTS COLLECTIVE
http://vacpoetry.org
ISBN-13: 978-0-9798825-6-2
ISBN-10: 0-9798825-6-7

Contents

序言, 李森   11

Preface, Li Sen   13

Single Cirrus, Wendy Barker   17

孤云, 温迪 · 巴克   17

我去过许多地方......, 李南   18

I have been in many places......, Li Nan   19

La Vida Nada, Jerry Bradley   20

虚空的生活, 杰里 · 布拉得雷   21

动荡不安的树叶, 李森   22

turbulent leaves, Li Sen   22

Thunder, Wendy Barker   23

雷鸣, 温迪 · 巴克   23

时光, 李南   24

time, Li Nan   25

In Celebration of Gray, Scott Wiggerman   26

庆祝灰色, 司各特 · 威格曼   27

故事和鸟群, 海男   28

stories and flocks of birds, Hai Nan   28

甘蔗林, 杨晓芸   29

sugarcane forest, Yang Xiaoyun   29

Quixote, Steven Schroeder   30

堂吉诃德, 史蒂文 · 施罗德   31

身体, 翟永明   32

bodies, Zhai Yongming   33

For Some Reason, Nathan Brown   36

因故, 内森 · 布朗   37

在古代, 翟永明   38

in ancient time, Zhai Yongming   39

This Alien Place Called Home, James Hoggard   42

这个叫作家的鬼地方, 詹姆斯 · 霍葛德   43

内衣的谜诀, 海男   44

the riddle of lingerie, Hai Nan   44

面对镜子, 海男   45

face to face with the mirror, Hai Nan   45

读李后主词仿十四行诗, 何小竹   46

in the manner of a sonnet, on reading lyric verse by Li Yu,
last monarch of Southern Tang, He Xiaozhu   47

The Family Secret, Natasha Marin   48

家庭秘密, 娜塔莎 · 马林   49

他们骂弯了清晨一米, 唐丹鸿   52

they shout abuses till early morning
bends one meter, Tang Danhong   53

Anniversary Trip, James Hoggard   54

周年纪念的旅程, 詹姆斯 · 霍葛德   55

梦见一个死于车祸的朋友, 刘春   58

dream of a friend who died in a car accident, Liu Chun   59

September, Scott Wiggerman   60

九月, 司各特 · 威格曼   60

回故里, 杨晓芸   61

going back to the old neighborhood, Yang Xiaoyun   61

October Revival in Texas, Scott Wiggerman   62

德克萨斯十月的复活, 司各特 · 威格曼   63

梦见苹果和鱼的安, 何小竹   64

dream of apples and fish, He Xiaozhu   65

Afterward, Jerry Bradley   66

之后, 杰里 · 布拉得雷   67

December, Aaron Rudolph   70

十二月, 阿龙 · 鲁道夫   71

Burn, Nathan Brown   72

燃烧, 内森 · 布朗   73

坟墓, 李森   74

grave, Li Sen   74

贪婪, 海男   75

greed, Hai Nan   75

A Note of Thanks, Nathan Brown   76

道谢便条, 内森 · 布朗   76

故乡, 李南   77

hometown, Li Nan   77

Dry Spell, David Meischen   78

干旱期, 大卫 · 麦森   79

Beyond the Entropy of Gophers, Jerry Craven   82

地鼠的混沌之外, 杰里·克莱文 83

声音和羽毛, 李森 84

sounds and feathers, Li Sen 84

Red-tailed Hawk, James Hoggard 85

红尾鹰, 詹姆斯·霍葛德 85

鸟群的声音, 海男 86

the flock's voice, Hai Nan 86

蝴蝶是怎样变成标本的, 海男 87

how a butterfly becomes a specimen, Hai Nan 87

鸟禽畜牲都好歌, 李森 88

song for the good birds and beasts, Li Sen 89

Mockingbird, Larry Thomas 92

水蒲苇莺, 赖里·托马斯 93

送一颗炮弹到喜玛拉雅山顶, 何小竹 94

shoot a bomb to the top of the Himalayas, He Xiaozhu 94

玻璃的味道, 海男 95

the flavor of glass, Hai Nan 95

Before the Coming of the Crow, Jerry Craven 96

乌鸦来临之前, 杰里·克莱文 97

漂亮的奴隶, 海男 98

a pretty slave, Hai Nan 98

Spring in Palo Duro Canyon, Jerry Craven 99

帕罗杜若峡谷的春天, 杰里·克莱文 99

躺在三天宽的歌喉上, 唐丹鸿 100

lie down on a voice singing three days wide, Tang Danhong 101

Condensation Nuclei, Wendy Barker 102

致密的核, 温迪·巴克 103

打开诗篇, 李南 104

break open psalms, Li Nan 105

Windmills, Sherry Craven 106

风车, 雪莉·克莱文 107

我写下的都是卑微的事物, 刘春 108

all I write about are insignificant things, Liu Chun 109

a nightingale risks, Natasha Marin 110

夜莺冒险, 娜塔莎·马林 111

这一天, 吉木狼格 112

this day, Jimu Langge 113

Holy is a fragile thing..., Sherry Craven 114

神圣是个纤弱的东西......，雪莉·克莱文 115

我就将爱上五月，黄芳 118

I will fall in love with May, Huang Fang 118

花儿，唐丹鸿 119

bloom, Tang Danhong 119

遥寄江南，李南 120

mail from the southern reaches of the Yangtze, Li Nan 121

Drink Water, Patricia Goodrich 122

饮水，帕特丽夏·古德里奇 123

私秘中的露台，海男 124

private balcony, Hai Nan 124

在广阔的世界上，李南 125

in the wide world, Li Nan 125

Grace Strokes, Kenneth Hada 126

优雅地划桨，肯尼斯·哈达 127

疼，李南 128

it hurts, Li Nan 129

Mirage, David Meischen 130

海市蜃楼，大卫·麦森 131

等待，冉仲景 132

waiting, Ran Zhongjing 132

那些花，杨晓芸 133

those flowers, Yang Xiaoyun 133

The Acuña Brothers Look North, 1952, Aaron Rudolph 134

阿库纳弟兄看北方，1952 年，阿龙·鲁道夫 135

五十年代的语言，翟永明 136

1950s language, Zhai Yongming 137

Gift, Alysa Hayes 140

礼物，艾莉莎·海斯 141

阿根廷蚂蚁，吉木狼格 142

Argentine ants, Jimu Langge 143

Midsummer Farewell, Jerry Craven 144

仲夏之别，杰里·克莱文 145

押韵是有瘾的，吉木狼格 146

rhyming is addictive, Jimu Langge 147

Blue in the Middle of a Corn Field, Alysa Hayes 148

玉米地里的忧伤, 艾莉莎·海斯 — 148

不是一头牛, 而是一群牛, 何小竹 — 149

not one head of cattle, but a herd of cattle, He Xiaozhu — 149

A Single Sheep, One Cow, Jerry Bradley — 150

一只绵羊, 一头牛, 杰里·布拉得雷 — 151

昆明的玫瑰, 李森 — 152

Kunming roses, Li Sen — 153

The Last Laugh, Alan Berecka — 154

最后一笑, 艾伦·巴拉克 — 155

平安夜, 黄芳 — 158

Christmas Eve, Huang Fang — 159

Our Lady, Patricia Goodrich — 160

我们的圣女, 帕特丽夏·古德里奇 — 160

桃花, 杨晓芸 — 161

peach blossom, Yang Xiaoyun — 161

毛妹, 店, 冉仲景 — 162

Mao Mei, shop, Ran Zhongjing — 163

Renovations at the Santuario de Guadalupe, Nathan Brown — 164

翻新德瓜达卢佩圣殿, 内森·布朗 — 165

Onion Creek, Fall, David Meischen — 166

洋葱河, 秋天, 大卫·麦森 — 166

庭院, 李森 — 167

courtyard, Li Sen — 167

train in the desert at night, Steven Schroeder — 168

行驶在沙漠夜色中的列车, 史蒂文·施罗德 — 169

卡夫卡, 刘春 — 170

Kafka, Liu Chun — 171

Downtown Albuquerque, Aaron Rudolph — 172

爱伯克奇市中心, 阿龙·鲁道夫 — 173

机关枪新娘, 唐丹鸿 — 174

machine gun bride, Tang Danhong — 175

Pastoral, Alysa Hayes — 176

田园, 艾莉莎·海斯 — 177

爱情和马, 吉木狼格 — 178

love and horse, Jimu Langge — 179

That Which Clings, Kenneth Hada — 180

那紧缠的, 肯尼斯·哈达 — 181

夸耀, 冉仲景   182

exaltation, Ran Zhongjing   183

West of Fort Worth, Scott Wiggerman   184

沃斯城堡以西, 司各特 · 威格曼   185

Blue Norther, Larry Thomas   186

蓝色北风, 赖里 · 托马斯   187

重阳登高, 翟永明   188

mountain climbing on double nine day, Zhai Yongming   189

摆手舞曲: 春天, 冉仲景   192

hand-waving dance: spring, Ran Zhongjing   192

prevailing time, Steven Schroeder   193

盛行的时令, 史蒂文 · 施罗德   193

债务, 冉仲景   194

debt, Ran Zhongjing   195

瓦蓝瓦蓝的天空, 李南   196

pastel blue sky, Li Nan   197

红土高原, 李森   198

red earth plateau, Li Sen   199

Low Pressure, Patricia Goodrich   200

低压, 帕特丽夏 · 古德里奇   200

当天晚上, 海男   201

that night, Hai Nan   201

色达草原, 何小竹   202

Seda Prairie, He Xiaozhu   203

Woody Guthrie Memorial Highway, Steven Schroeder   204

树木茂密的高斯里公路, 史蒂文 · 施罗德   205

almost human, Steven Schroeder   206

近乎人类, 史蒂文 · 施罗德   206

西昌的月亮, 吉木狼格   207

Xichang moon, Jimu Langge   207

Full Moon, Cirrocumulus, Light Breeze,
and Iridescence, Wendy Barker   208

满月、卷积云、清风和虹彩, 温迪 · 巴克   209

虚构的玫瑰, 海男   210

illusive roses, Hai Nan   210

干燥的南部山冈, 海男   211

dry, dry southern hills, Hai Nan   211

Near-Earth Object, Wendy Barker 212

临近地球的物体, 温迪·巴克 213

Harvest Moon, Larry Thomas 214

满月, 赖里·托马斯 215

减法, 冉仲景 216

subtraction, Ran Zhongjing 216

到底是谁出卖了我, 海男 217

who sold me out in the end? Hai Nan 217

仿佛这忧伤, 黄芳 218

as if this sadness, were real, Huang Fang 219

Kite Flying, Sherry Craven 220

断线的风筝, 雪莉·克莱文 221

Cleaving a Valentine, Jerry Bradley 222

情人节的断肠人, 杰里·布拉得雷 223

Winter Wedding, Alan Berecka 224

冬日婚礼, 艾伦·巴拉克 225

Yu's Wife, Natasha Marin 226

禹的妻子, 娜塔莎·马林 227

Nobody's Sugar Daddy Now, David Meischen 228

现在落单的甜爹, 大卫·麦森 229

a section from

Games, Alysa Hayes 230

节选自《游戏》, 艾莉莎·海斯 231

Dust Storm, Larry Thomas 232

沙尘暴, 赖里·托马斯 233

Translations 234

Afterword – On *Two Southwests*, Steven Schroeder 241

后记——关于《两个西南》, 史蒂文·施罗德 243

Contributors 247

Index of Poems by Author 259

序 言

李森

　　无论在中国还是在美国，西南地区都处于话语中心之外的边缘。无论在历史还是在现实的文化境遇中，边缘都是最具有生命力的地带。中心常常意味着垂死和腐朽。因为在中心，文化成规通常被视为正当，在这种所谓正当性的荒谬体系之中，寄生着各种文化形态的利益集团，包括诗歌创作和批评的利益集团。利益集团为了维护自己的利益，必然将边缘的思想、文化及其创造力或视为异端，或视而不见。自古以来，消解中心，甚至可以说是拯救中心的文化沉沦，阻止中心的文化暴力，都是处在边缘的有识之士的历史责任。因此，包括诗人在内的一批批文化精英都会带着边缘野性的、源生的创造力和激情，去维护自己的话语权力，保护自己的天赋才能，创造文化丰富多彩的可能性。任何时代，任何国家，在一种文化形态取代另一种文化形态，形成彼时"当代"潮流的过程中，边缘的人物和思想都起着决定性的作用。异端摧毁成规，激情催生良知，正义塑造心智。来自边缘的诗歌的正义，义无反顾地创造诗歌的"当代"和未来。

　　《两个西南》是"昆明—芝加哥小组"部分成员编选的一部诗集，这部诗集选译了美国西南地区和中国西南地区一部分当下诗人的作品。其中，许多诗人是美国和中国当代的著名诗人。这本诗集得以出版，主要有赖史蒂文·施罗德博士的策划和为编辑、出版所付出的努力，许多诗人和译者参与了这个项目的工作，付出了辛劳。这部诗集以英语和汉语双语出版，使诗歌作品尽可能为阅读保持了原作的风貌，也为研究者提供了方便。诗是很难翻译的，无数诗人都对诗歌的翻译提出过质疑。不过，我们所做的工作已经表明了一种立场，或一种事实：诗歌从一种语言转化为另一种语言的过程中，仍然会形成意想不到的诗意的惊喜，呈现出卓越的诗歌文本。这样的文本屡见不鲜，是精神和文化交流成为可能的明证。这一事实需要我们来重新廓清翻译的观念。窃以为，诗歌翻译与诗歌阅读一样，都是一种对原作的创造。事实当然是，任何阅读都不能复原原作，翻译也是如此。即便诗人自己，面对自己的诗作，也常常在误读中引申或消解了诗歌的所谓原意。伟大的诗歌文本，从来都只创作了一个可靠出发点，哪怕这个出发点是多么的自足和直观，如钻石般有晶莹剔透的自在开显，也只能像猫头鹰的眼睛一样，是看者的出发点，又是被看者的出发点。诗在亲近和误读中形成，也在

11

亲近和误读中解放。在这个意义上来看诗歌翻译，我们就有足够的理由相信诗的翻译作为一种创作的巨大贡献。尽管翻译者在面对母语之外的另外一种语言时，都有不同程度的尴尬，但大家都像磨砺刀锋一样磨砺每一个词，每一个句子。有时候，花费一天的时间都不能译完一首短诗，不过，当一首好诗在语言转化中变成了另一首好诗的时候，翻译的快乐也是难以言表的。为诗的创作和翻译付出时间、精力的代价，并乐此不疲，是精神贵族的事业。尤其像王浩、龙晓滢等这般青年才俊，他们很少写诗或不写诗，但他们的翻译工作是那样尽心尽力，从无怨言，随叫随到，不计得失，他们在其他方面也乐于助人，对他人甚至比对自己更好。我常常被他们的个人品质所打动，在我的眼里，包括史蒂文·施罗德、张晓红等人士在内的、我所认识的精神贵族，都是在日常生活中可以信任、艺术生活中可以同行的大丈夫。当然，还有那些我暂时陌生的翻译家和诗人，我已在阅读他们的原作和译作的每一个时刻亲近他们。年复一年，日复一日，我都在与惺惺相惜者同行，学习人性中熠熠生辉的品质。在跨越国界的文化、诗歌视野中，我仍然蔑视自私，歌颂人世间的道义。

2008-07-31

12

Preface

The southwest region, in China as in the US, is the periphery far from the center of discourse. The periphery, however, is the most vigorous in both historical and present cultural circumstances. The center is often associated with impending death and decadence, because cultural conventions are often legitimized here. Interest groups in various cultural forms, including those engaged in poetry writing and criticism, parasitize such an absurd but legitimized system. To protect their interest, they must treat peripheral ideas and cultures as heretical, or just ignore them. It has been the responsibility of those well-informed in the periphery to decentralize the center, or rather to save it from its cultural decadence, and to prevent its cultural violence. Cultural elites including poets will take advantage of their peripheral, untamed, and original creativity and passion to protect their talent and right of discourse, and to create multiple possibilities of culture. In any time and in any country, peripheral people and thoughts always have a decisive role to play when one culture replaces another to create a "contemporary" trend of its time. The heretical destroy conventions, passion catalyzes conscience, and justice shapes the human mind. Justice of poetry, as arises in the periphery, courageously creates the "present" and future.

Two Southwests is an anthology compiled by some members of the Kunming-Chicago Group. It is a bilingual collection of poems by some well-known contemporary poets from the southwest regions of China and the US. This anthology would not have been possible without Steven Schroeder's painstaking efforts to design, edit, and print it. Many poets and translators have participated in this project and made their contributions. This collection, published in both Chinese and English, is meant to help the reader access the original when reading the translations, and to help the critics with their studies. Poems are hard to translate, and numerous poets have doubted the translatability of poetry. What we have done, however, is an expression of a stand or the fact that the conversion of poetry from one language to another may bring poetic surprises and produce outstanding lines. Such lines are frequently seen, which testifies to the possibility of spiritual and cultural communication. Such a fact imposes the job on us to redefine translation. I believe that poetry translation and reading are a process of re-creation. The fact is, of course, neither poetry reading nor poetry translation can reconstruct the original meaning. When reading one's own poems, even the poet is often lost in misinterpretation and over-interpretation, dissolving the so-called original meaning. Great lines provide nothing but a reliable starting-point, no matter how self-sufficient or self-evident. Even if a great line is as crystal-clear as a diamond, it can only serve as a starting-point, like an owl's eyes, for the seeing and the seen. Poetry comes into being in intimacy and misinterpretation; it is emancipated in intimacy and misinterpretation. Viewing from such a perspective, we have a good reason to acknowledge the great contributions made by poetry translation as a form of creation. Although every translator feels some kind of awkwardness when facing a language other than his or her mother tongue, she or he hones each word and sentence the way one would hone a knife. Sometimes one day is not enough time to translate a short poem, but the joy of fulfillment is just inexpressible when a good poem is turned into another good poem in a different language. It is an enterprise of spiritual aristocrats to invest time and energy in poetry writing and translation. Talented young people like Wang Hao and Long Xiaoying, who write few poems, are committed to translation and are always available when they are needed; they work without complaints or calculation of losses and gains; they are always ready to help others, treating people better than themselves. Steven Schroeder and Zhang Xiaohong are the spiritual aristocrats I know. They are great friends in my life and great companions in my journey of art: they are heroes. Of course there are those poets and translators I do not know in person, but I am in a spiritual communion with them whenever I read their poems and translations. Year in year out and day in day out, I travel with kindred souls and learn those noble qualities of human nature. In the moments of cultural and poetry communication across countries, I despise selfishness and celebrate justice.

Li Sen
31 July 2008
Kunming, Yunnan

Single Cirrus
Wendy Barker

The flotilla out of sight,
a smidgen, dash,
a skiff, canoe, isolate
kayak that skims
the lake on a whiff,
breeze, aspiration
of the h in hello, a hand
extended, fingers unfolded,
lips puckered for a shy
kiss, more to come.

孤云
温迪·巴克

远逝的舰队，
星星点点，
小帆船、独木舟、
小艇孤独地飘浮在湖面上
像一阵风
微风就是那"HELLO"中"H"的发音
轻盈地送去我由衷的牵挂
伸出的手，伸直的手指
双唇嘟起，接受一个羞涩的
吻，下面更精彩。

我去过许多地方……
李南

我去过许多地方：庄稼连着农舍
白天接着黑夜。
篱笆上晾晒的花衣
妇女们在房顶簸谷或选豆
黄牛俯下身去，在水渠边喝水
呵，它在啜饮土地无边的灾难

我独爱这个地理的中国
是因为我没有去过别的国家。

我爱落日下方的坑沟
也爱各种方言、农民干活儿的姿势
一棵草草斜过它的身体
几座坟茔，让远逝的人群与大地平行。

这就是我的祖国：
迷信和战争走过它每一寸肌肤
这就是我的人民：
在风中，他们命若琴弦

I have been in many places......
Li Nan

I have been in many places: crops link farmhouses
day follows night.
Flowery clothes dry in sunshine on fences
women winnow grain, sort beans
ocher ox bends, drinks beside canal
oh, it drinks earth's boundless suffering

I love the lay of China's land
because I have never traveled elsewhere.

I love the sunset on that ditch
and I love every dialect, the posture of peasants working
the angle of bending grass
a few burial mounds, people fading in the distance

this is indeed my motherland:
superstition and war stalk every inch of its skin
these are indeed my people:
in the wind, lives like reeds

La Vida Nada
Jerry Bradley

my dreams burn like green chili
but still play hard to get
my ambition barely acknowledges
its own presence in the mirror

my flirtation with success
is never taken seriously
let's just be friends
she repeats whenever I call

pennies fall through my pockets
like the holes were carved-out cantaloupes
paper money won't keep out the cold

my father's belt, the one that wore
me out when I didn't get A's,
barely keeps me tied to my own ass

the future predicts little lost lies,
holds my horoscope hostage
on aberrational parchment

my career, too paramilitary,
sits in fatigues ready to blow me away
with no remorse for its terror

disease has already set foot
on my basement stair
flies gather around the hole
in my open fantasy

when anyone asks how I died
just say I strangled on my potential

虚空的生活

杰里·布拉得雷

我的梦想像青椒一样炽烈
但仍然难以实现
我的野心，几乎不承认
它在镜中的存在

我与成功的调情
从未被当真
每当我表白，她都重复着
我们做普通朋友吧

硬币从我的口袋里掉落
好像那洞孔是挖空的甜瓜
纸币也不能御寒

我爸爸的腰带，让我疲惫
在我没得 A 时
简直绑不紧我自个儿的屁股

未来预告着极少迷途的谎言，
把我的星象扣押
在离经叛道的羊皮纸上做人质

我的岁月，过于准军事化
穿着士兵工作服准备把我炸飞
对于它的恐怖，无怨无悔

疾病已经踏上
我地下室的楼梯
在我敞开的幻想中
苍蝇聚集在洞口周围

要是有人问我如何死去
就说我被自身的潜力憋死

动荡不安的树叶
李森

动荡不安的树叶，总是动荡不已
不会离开枝头，也不会折断树枝
我看见它们把所有的鸟类都藏在山的怀里
把麂子马鹿也藏在山的怀里
动荡不安的树叶，从来不会让我看见一头豹子
也不会把果子装进我的箩筐
假如我是一片树叶
我也不会离开树枝，离开万千沟壑
因为时间还不到，果子还不成熟
但总有那么一天，我会落下来
我还会模仿其他的树叶，重新长出来

turbulent leaves
Li Sen

turbulent leaves, endlessly agitated
will not leave the bough, will not break it
I see every bird in mountain's embrace
barking deer, red deer in mountain's embrace
turbulent leaves, will not let me see a panther
or put fruit in my basket
if I were a leaf
I wouldn't leave the bough either, leave ten thousand ravines
for the time has not come, fruit has not ripened
but the day will come, I will fall down
I will imitate leaves, grow again

Thunder
Wendy Barker

To Descartes, one cloud falling
onto another. To the Greeks,
Zeus's shield shaking, a forerunner
of Hopkins' shook foil, that grandeur,
gathered and charged. For the native
tribes of the plains, Thunderbird's
wings beating. Such magnified
oscillations are beyond us, yet
the very air we breathe is grumbling,
a succession of compressions,
negative and positive ions colliding,
as someone in the next room
is about to explode.

雷鸣
温迪 · 巴克

对于笛卡儿而言，一朵云彩落在
一朵云彩上。对于希腊人而言，
这会儿宙斯的盾在颤动，一个霍普金斯的先行者
正在挥动利剑，那壮观的场面，
集合，向前冲。
对于平原上的土著部落，雷鸟的翅膀
拍打着。如此巨大的振荡
让我们无法理喻，可是
我们所呼吸的空气正轰隆作响，
一连串的压缩，
正负极离子相互撞击，
犹如隔壁房间的什么人
即将爆发。

时光
李南

它带走河流,带走事物的瞬间
却徒然地留下了我们!
这么多年,我们停留在安泰的年份
见证着又一批人出游四海
时光啊,痛苦的黄金!
使我们蒙受恩典,欢乐或者绝望.
这么多年,我们找不到永恒的方向
在错误的花卉中
一次次丧失

就是这些时光,这些无形的黄金
使万物黯淡
教我们衰老的心愿不再回转
这些时光啊,满载人间的平民
让他们消亡,象流水一般远逝
这些时光
只留下英雄和大师,他们不朽
微风吹动的脸庞徐徐呈现
在夜空中,在多少年后

time
Li Nan

it takes away rivers, takes away things in a twinkling
leaves us empty!
in this way, we sojourn many years in peace
witness crowds of people passing through the world again
oh time, made gold by pain!
it makes us suffer kindness, happy or hopeless
so many years, we cannot find lasting direction
in the wrong flowers
once time is lost

these times invisible gold indeed
make the ten thousand things pale
teach our old feeble desires not to return
these times, oh, the world a vehicle packed with common folk
let them die, like running water dies in the distance
these times
leave only heroes and masters, immortal
gentle breeze slowly rises brushes faces appears
in night sky after how many years

In Celebration of Gray
Scott Wiggerman

An iris blooms in crisp white robes.
Temperatures hover near eighty.
All winter the sun shone like June—

until today
when skies are dishwater-gray,
cold scampers through cracks under doors,
and the furnace at last is on.

And rain—
the slow, steady, soaking kind
that's avoided Texas like a mother-in-law—

plasters leaves to sidewalks.
Soil actually looks moist;
the undersides of limbs are wet.
Trees suddenly stand out, naked

against the gray swath of a horizon
that will not last
but finally feels right.

庆祝灰色

司各特·威格曼

一株鸢尾像清新的白袍开了花。
温度在八十度上下摇摆。
整个冬天艳阳高照如同六月——

直到今天
天空如刷锅水般灰暗，
寒冷从门缝里窜过，
暖炉终于点上了。

而雨——
徐徐的，持续的和湿透的那种
避开德克萨斯就像躲避婆婆——

把叶子涂抹在人行道上。
土壤居然看似湿润；
树枝下面是潮湿的。
树木猛然凸现，光秃秃的

对着一条灰色的地平线
它不会持久
但最终恰到好处。

故事和鸟群

海男

天突然阴郁，层层的风季
微薄的冰雪从未来临，但是，骨头却彻底冰冷了
骨头里的节奏。知识和罪恶都朝着一个方向
在这晶莹的恐怖里，故事和鸟群
都将一双翅膀紧紧抓住
看见了更加糊涂透顶的马群
往山坡的殉葬地奔去。这种目的地
使人更加回忆群星在一架天平上
统治了这虚无，谦逊的大地上，饱满的生命
而他们吁出的气，压抑，拆散了屋梁
连最小的婴儿也不知道怎么办
在纯洁的花蕾存在时怎么办

stories and flocks of birds

Hai Nan

Sky grows dark, season of wind layered on wind
ice and snow have not come, but bones are cold as ice
rhythm in bone. Crime and knowledge go the same direction
in this crystalline terror, stories and flocks of birds
both fold wings tight
they saw more muddle-headed horses
galloping toward the hillside burial ground. Such destinations
make people think of the stars on a balance
governing this emptiness, on modest ground, lives full
breath depressed, roof beams splitting
even the smallest child has no idea what to do
when pure flower buds exist what to do

甘蔗林
杨晓芸

几个小媳妇，站在甘蔗林
声音甜美
我有花纸的糖果吃
我叫她们姨
这些老美人，如今坐在院坝里
着青色棉袄，吐瓜皮儿
如同秋风走过甘蔗林

sugarcane forest
Yang Xiaoyun

a few young wives stand near the sugarcane forest
voices sweet
I have these fancy paper candies
I call them auntie
these old beauties, now sit in the courtyard
wear black cotton jackets, spit melon skins
like autumn wind passing sugarcane forest

Quixote
Steven Schroeder

The pull of an old
wooden windmill and
a ramshackle shack fifty
miles from Tucumcari
reminds me that I am
a child of Quixote. My
father carried a camera
the way the knight
carried a lance.

       He would see
giants there to slay with clouds
against skies so blue they'd
make a knight of Sancho
and melt Dulcinea's heart.

堂吉诃德

史蒂文·施罗德

一架老式木头风车的转动
和离图卡姆卡里十五英里
摇摇欲坠的小木棚
使我想起我是一个
少年堂吉诃德。
我父亲总是带着照相机
好像骑士携着长矛。

        他仿佛看见
巨人们正在那儿与云朵联手
残害蓝澄澄的天空
他们想造就桑丘骑士
并融化杜尔西内娅的心。

身体
翟永明

这对身体被酒渍过了
现在 它们冒出一股甜味
酒渍过的虾、蟹
还有那些渍过的话题、追问
香菜和眼神
都已落到身体的底部
又被那里已埋了三十年的酒淹没

从此 它们象鱼一样
在这对玻璃身体里来回游
来回吐泡 交欢
来回发酵 许多年过去
它们又变成陈酿

这对身体现在抬起来
又落下去 还是没能
把身体里的醉空出来
其中一个身体渍得较多
它倒给另一个
另一个身体很快也醉了
很快地溢了出来

那些溢出来的酒也被渍过了
被他们的汗味、皮肤味
唇腔味 还有一些复杂的体味
渍过了 从身体的各个毛孔泛出
那些酒变得很怪 很呛人

也许多年过去
这对身体更加透明
他们内部的草呵根呵
都全部沉落瓶底
它们所需要的醇度

bodies
Zhai Yongming

the twinned bodies have been soaked in wine
now   they emit a sweet scent
wine-soaked shrimps, crabs
saturated topics, inquiries
coriander and the expression in one's eyes
all fall into the bottom of the bodies
also submerged by the wine that has been buried there
                                                    for thirty years

since then   like fish they
swim back and forth in twinned glass bodies
round and round emit bubbles   copulate
round and round ferment   till years later
they turn once more into fine vintage

the twinned bodies now rise
and then fall   still unable
to clear the intoxication
one of the bodies more saturated
pours some for the other
which soon gets drunk
and overflows

the spilt wine is soaked as well
with the smell of their sweat, skin
taste of lips   some complex savor
saturates   oozing out of various pores
the wine gets very strange   very pungent

perhaps years later
these twinned bodies even more crystalline
their inner grasses and roots
will all sink to the bottom of the bottle
the degree of mellowness they need

就是这样勾兑
这对身体
从此不再喝其它的酒

is thus deepened
these twinned bodies
drink no more wine

For Some Reason
Nathan Brown

I watch the 8 p.m. sun
throw shadows from ivy
onto red clay brick just
before summer storm clouds
wrap around the light, as if
they're tired of its heat
bullying us on August nights.

These small atmospheric kindnesses
remind me of the unsolvable
mystery of my love for Oklahoma.

Boston, Carmel... Santa Fe, Colorado
Springs... I'll go any chance I get.
But these places are
the beautiful girl
you're afraid to know
too well, because...

because this is home,
and I'll probably stay
right here
right where
my enemies will always
know they can find me.

因故

内森·布朗

我注视着晚上八点钟的太阳
就在夏季的暴风云
吞噬这光亮之前
把常春藤的影子
撒在红土砖上
它们仿佛厌倦了太阳的热度
在八月的夜晚威吓着我们。

这些微弱而朦胧的善意
使我想起那不解之谜——
我对俄克拉荷马的爱

波士顿、卡梅尔……圣达菲、科罗拉多
斯布林斯[1]……我一逮着机会就去走走。
但这些地方
是那你不敢深交的
漂亮姑娘
因为……

因为这儿便是家，
我大概就是要待在
这个地方
待在这个我的宿敌
总能找到我的地方。

---

[1]   译者注：地名，位于科罗拉多州。

在古代
翟永明

在古代，我只能这样
给你写信　并不知道
我们下一次
会在哪里见面

现在　我往你的邮箱
灌满了群星　它们都是五笔字形
它们站起来　为你奔跑
它们停泊在天上的某处
我并不关心

在古代　青山严格地存在
当绿水醉倒在他的脚下
我们只不过抱一抱拳　彼此
就知道后会有期

现在，你在天上飞来飞去
群星满天跑　碰到你就象碰到疼处
它们象无数的补丁　去堵截
一个蓝色屏幕　它们并不歇斯底里

在古代　人们要写多少首诗？
才能变成崂山道士　穿过墙
穿过空气　再穿过一杯竹叶青
抓住你　更多的时候
他们头破血流　倒地不起

现在　你正拨一个手机号码
它发送上万种味道
它灌入了某个人的体香
当某个部位颤抖　全世界都颤抖

in ancient time
Zhai Yongming

in ancient time, I could only write like this
letters to you   not knowing
where our next meeting
would be

now   I pour into your mailbox
a constellation of stars   all written in five strokes
they stand up   run for you
they berth somewhere in the sky
I don't care

in ancient time   blue mountains did exist
when green waters groveled at his feet
we just saluted each other with fists folded and raised   both
knowing we'd meet again

now, you flit to and fro in the sky
the constellation runs everywhere   bumps into you like
touching a sore spot
like patches   they go blocking up
a blue screen   and they are not hysteric

in ancient time   how many poems did they have to write?
to become Laoshan Daoist priests   who passed through walls
passed through air   passed through a glass of bamboo-green liqueur
to capture you   but more often
they bled all over   collapsing on the ground

now   you dial a cellphone number
it transmits ten thousand flavors
it is saturated with someone's smell
when some part trembles   the whole world trembles

在古代　我们并不这样
我们只是并肩策马　走几十里地
当耳环叮当作响　你微微一笑
低头间　我们又走了几十里地

in ancient time   we didn't live this way
we just rode horses side by side   traveling miles
when your earrings jingled   you faintly smiled
head down   we traveled more miles in the meantime

This Alien Place Called Home
James Hoggard

There are no antique shards to dig up here
Because the winds had blown the gods away
the Indians dared not set their camps near here,

and now we have to face the fact that where
we live has no tradition, nothing's stayed:
there are no antique shards to dig up here

If we in foolishness created where
we live, we never cared in any way
the Indians dared not set their camps near here –

unless, thinking, we start to wonder: Were
they right? And yes, they might have been, so say:
There are no antique shards to dig up here

then ask if our own fathers did not hear
the message of the winds and droughts, that they,
the Indians dared not set their camps near here,

and then admit our fathers were wild-haired
and driven – staking claims, they did not say:
There are no antique shards to dig up here
The Indians dared not set their camps near here

这个叫作家的鬼地方

詹姆斯 · 霍葛德

这里挖不出先辈们遗迹的碎片
因为神灵已随风而逝
印第安人不敢在这附近宿营，

我们的住地没有过去，什么都没有留下——
这是我们须要面对的事实
这里挖不出先辈们遗迹的碎片

如果我们在愚昧中创造了我们的住地
我们半点也不在意
印第安人不敢在这附近宿营

除非，想想吧，我们开始纳闷：
先辈的做法是否正确？啊，是的，或许他们是对的，故曰：
这里挖不出先辈们遗迹的碎片

接下来问问我们的先辈是否听不见
这风与干旱的讯息，而他们，那些
印第安人不敢在这附近宿营

之后承认我们的父辈蓬头垢面，颇感紧迫——
在这里安营扎寨，而他们没有说：
这里挖不出先辈们遗迹的碎片
印第安人不敢在这附近宿营

内衣的谜诀
海男

每一层内衣的谜诀都已经附在
体外，因而，紧贴住了那些肉色中的
窗口，我们守候着这些密封的窗口
不允许外在的敌人撕开这谜诀

也许已经选择了最柔软的棉花
删除完毕了黑暗中的歌曲
首先，她身体上的内衣
是她个人的，是她遭遇到的风格

她选择了红色、紫色或粉色
恪守住了她每个阶段的热情
她送走了令她厌倦的伙伴
她剔除并抛弃了生命中并不柔软的时光

the riddle of lingerie
Hai Nan

every layer of lingerie a riddle attached
to the skin, clinging close to those flesh-colored
windows, those sealed windows we guard
from outside enemies who try to tear the riddles open

perhaps the softest cotton was selected
songs in the dark deleted
first, her lingerie
is her own style, the style she encounters

she chooses red, purple, perhaps pink
maintains her passion at every stage
sends dreary companions away
dumps those times in her life that are not so soft

面对镜子
海男

又单独面对镜子，影响一种真实可靠的声音
在镜子里，我面对惊奇和狂喜的东西
用一只鸟的归来代替水平线上的春天
用镜子统于阿尔卑斯山上的大雪
大雪和白色，一件具体的、个别的事物
一种不偏不倚的方法在镜子中适用于狡猾的平面
从一般的脸庞上，面目的吸吮中
遵循我对镜子的反抗和从容的决心
黑夜从我三岁的故乡山冈上看见我的镜子
在内心接受的教育中，镜子在困难中
淘汰我对黑暗的害怕，造成了另一种局面
不能离开镜子，它特殊的地位又限制了我

face to face with the mirror
Hai Nan

Alone again face to face with the mirror, affecting a real and
                                              reliable voice
in the mirror, I face something amazing and wild
use the return of a bird to stand for Spring above the horizon
use the mirror to control heavy snow on the Alps
heavy snow and the color white, concrete, particular
an even-handed method in the mirror is useful on tricky surfaces
the ordinary faces, faces drawn
I resist the mirror with calm resolution
on a dark night when I was three I faced the mirror on the low hills
                                              of my home
through the inner education received, the mirror with difficulty
overcomes my fear of darkness, makes it so
I can't live without a mirror, its uniqueness confines me

读李后主词仿十四行诗

何小竹

注释里说，雕栏玉砌的宫廷
跟人民没有什么关系
他的哀愁只是亡国之君个人的哀愁
但注释者笔锋一转，又说
他擅长将过去与现在
紧密地扣在一起
平常的话语用得十分鲜活
春花秋月何时了，就是这首词
如果让我写一篇赏析
我可能无话可说
无话可说，惟有原封不动
将它抄录一遍

问君能有几多愁
恰似一江春水向东流

in the manner of a sonnet, on reading lyric verse by Li Yu, last monarch of Southern Tang
He Xiaozhu

the annotator says, carved balustrades of the royal palace
have nothing to do with the masses
his lament is only the lament of a monarch deposed
yet the annotator changes his tone, saying
he is good too at
linking past to present
with his innovative use of common discourse
when will Spring blossoms and Autumn moon end, is
                                 the verse *per se*
if I am asked to write a comment
I will probably have nothing to say
nothing to say, but transcribe it
verbatim

how much worry can a ruler bear
like a Spring river of east-bound water

The Family Secret
Natasha Marin

1.   My mother says she found
just one Trinidad dollar in my pocket.
The ink had printed a lonely red bird
onto my palm.

2.   Four-year-old girls
need to be supervised. They have barely
thinned into girls—baby cheeks still turn
to moons when she sleeps. She is not a baby
except to her mother, who watches her sleeping
       and aches to hold her
         to her breast again.

Hours later she turned up at school.
We asked her where she had gone.
She lied.

To this day, we don't know where she went.
Little girl. Disappeared. For hours.

3.   Trinidad dollar red
red the color of her nail polish pinching red
red smiling red kissing red holding red
my hand red
my dress red
my scream crimson red
and curdling red red
red the color of my own blood red
red the color of my open wrists red
red the color of a fist through a window red
like red skin sliced away circumcision red
red the tight choke of color at my throat,
red the color of his breath at my forehead red

家庭秘密
娜塔莎·马林

1、 我的妈妈说她在我的口袋里
只发现了一元特立尼达岛钞票。
油墨在我的手掌中印下
一只红色的孤独的鸟。

2、 四岁的女孩子
需要监督。她们只不过
抽条 成女孩——她睡觉时
孩子的脸还是朝着月亮。对妈妈来说
她还是个小孩儿，妈妈看着她睡觉
　　忍着疼痛，又一次
　　把她抱到胸前。

几个小时后，她在学校出现
我们问她去了什么地方。
她撒了谎。

这一天，我们不知道她去了哪儿。
小女孩。消失。几个小时。

3、 特立尼达货币是红色的
红色是她的指甲涂上了淡淡的红色
红色的微笑红色的吻红色的拥抱红色
我的手是红色的
我的衣裳是红色的
我的尖叫声是血红色的
红色的凝结是红色的
血液红色是我自己血液的颜色
红色是割破手腕便泛出的颜色
红色是砸向玻璃的拳头的颜色
宛如割礼中被切掉的红色皮肤的颜色
红色是紧紧扼住喉咙的颜色
红色是他呼在我前额的气息的颜色

red the color of the weapon and the wound red
red the moon, red the flow, red the ebbing edge of red
red the exact color of the bison tracing red in ochre red in blood
red the color of caves, wombs, lips—red frills of memory
red earth gritty against your white teeth red
red like fire like rage like war like danger like warning red
the giant red blinking no no no no no no no of red

There is no red that red.

红色武器和伤口的颜色
红色的月亮，红色的潮涨潮落，边缘的颜色
红色已变成被激怒的野牛要冲向的颜色，沉淀在赭石和血液中的色彩
红色染红了洞穴、源起、嘴唇——记忆中红色的片断
比起你洁白的牙齿红色的牙龈更加坚韧
红色就是那火、那愤怒、那战争、那危险、那红色的警报
巨大的红色闪烁着红色的不不不不不不不

没有红色那样地红

他们骂弯了清晨一米

唐丹鸿

他们骂弯了清晨一米，
我在幼芽的高度抽泣。
这不关太阳的事，朝霞，
照样任裙子烂掉。
他们骂我。

我骂飞了春天。
绝育梦，盛满乳房的冰雪。
这不关他们的事，
他们吸吮着，痛苦地
堕去我腹中的花。

花骂美了现实。
太阳弯曲着清晨打我。
手从太阳的高度打我的破碎。
太阳之手打我的朝霞。
这不关我的事。
幼芽在一米五的夜烂掉。
冰雪隆起我的胸部。
花隆起了他们。
春天恳求我原谅。

这时，我活不下去了，
一边哭，一边嗅，一边蹲下，
任他们摸疼痛的星空。

这不关爱的事。

星空失去其痛，
星空是我吗？

they shout abuses till early morning bends one meter
Tang Danhong

they shout abuses till early morning bends one meter,
I weep at the height of the seedling.
this doesn't concern the sun, rosy dawn,
lets the skirt rot as ever.
they shout abuses at me.

I shout abuses till spring flies away.
dreams about sterilization, breasts full of ice and snow.
this doesn't concern them,
sucking, with pain
they abort the bloom in my belly.

bloom shouts abuses till reality becomes beautiful.
sun bends early morning to beat me.
from the height of the sun hand shatters my fragments.
sun's hand shatters my rosy dawn.
this doesn't concern me.
the seedling rots on the one and a half meter evening.
ice and snow swell my breasts.
the bloom swells them.
spring begs my forgiveness.

at this moment, I cannot live on,
weeping, smelling, squatting,
letting them stroke the aching starry night.

this doesn't concern love.

the starry night loses its pain,
is the starry night me?

Anniversary Trip
James Hoggard

It was not evil, though it looked that way,
the copperhead wrapped round a branch
four feet from our eyes by the Brazos,
a river once called Arms of God

After beaching our canoe for lunch
we had lain on a slope on the bank
then moved to a clearing for shade

where a breeze, sliding coolly now
through our loosened clothes,
fingered its way across us,

a salt cedar brake and scrub oak mott
screening us from public view

Letting skin see in its own oblique way,
I let my gaze drift, but my breath
disappeared, my eyes now locked
on an oddly long knot

twisted on a branch twisted before us,
and the dark ragged bands were not wood,
and the shotlike red eyes did not blink

Look straight ahead, I said, *don't move*

And fingernails now biting blood
from our palms, we rose,
and the brush seemed to watch us,
as slowly we moved away

周年纪念的旅程

詹姆斯·霍葛德

一条铜头蛇面目狰狞，但并不邪恶
缠绕着一根树枝，
在布拉鲁斯旁离我们眼睛四英尺的地方
那条曾被叫作上帝之臂的河流

我们划着独木舟上岸去吃午饭
躺在岸边的斜坡上
之后又移到空地上躲阴凉

那里微风轻拂，凉凉的，
溜进我们解开的衣服里，
如手指拂过我们

海生雪松和矮小的橡胶林
让我们与世隔绝

让皮肤用它自己模棱两可的方式去感受，
让我的目光漂逝，可我的呼吸
渐渐消失，而我的眼睛正死死地盯着
一个奇怪的长长的结

它在我们面前与扭曲的树枝扭曲在一起，
那黑黢黢参差不齐的条状物并不是树木，
充血的眼睛没有眨动

向前看，我说，别动

现在，指甲咬着
掌心流出的血，我们起身
慢慢离开的时候
灌木丛似乎注视着我们。

in a way we have not always done,
memory saying we'd see that snake
everywhere we looked the rest of the day

我们离开的方式并不常见
记忆告诉我们，我们将在这天余下的时间里
处处看见那条蛇。

梦见一个死于车祸的朋友
刘春

许多年了，我不止一次经过那个地方
仿佛去看一部没有结局的旧电影
金属镜架把他的鼻子压得很低
笑容随意，不说话
又仿佛有什么东西秘而不宣

生活随意的男人，圈子里知名的
花花大少。从他的脸色看不出
几分钟后的恐惧、绝望
和对尘世难以言表的眷恋
唉，这个世界所有的形容词也描述不了
几分钟后汽车来临时的突然

一切都毫无征兆——
我和未婚妻上街，买席梦思
他勾着一个女人的脖子，在对街
朝我大喊大叫，笑容带着纵欲后的疲倦
和找到归属般的温情

"要结婚了。无论是谁都应该结婚
好好地爱一个女人。因为
那是你幸福的根源。"我注意到
他说话时，左手抬了抬鼻梁上的镜架

一个性格众所周知的男人，在某个特定场合
对另一个他所了解的男人说一些
违心的话语，是可以理解的
而我多么后悔当时的参与——
"是的，花心的男人，迟早会被汽车撞死。"

dream of a friend who died in a car accident
Liu Chun

For many years, I passed through that place incessantly
as though watching an old movie that will not end
the metal frame of his glasses pressed down low on his nose
smiling complacently, not speaking
as though there were some secret not to be publicly divulged

a playboy, well-known in the neighborhood
few great tears. See within from his look
after a few minutes of fear, despair
difficult to feel between the lines for the dust of life
O, every adjective in this world is unable to describe
moments later the car suddenly appears

no sign at all——
a fiancee I take to the street, buy a mattress
he rests an arm on a woman's shoulder, across the street
he shouts to me, smiles a tired lecherous
tender smile as if he had a sense of belonging

"You must marry. No matter whom everyone should marry
earnestly love some woman. Because
that is the origin of happiness." I listen
when he speaks, his left hand lifting the frame of his glasses on
his nose

A man personally known to all who, on a particular occasion,
says words against his will
to another man he knows. This is understandable
but how I regret being present——
"Yes, sooner or later, a womanizer will be hit by a car."

September
Scott Wiggerrman

Erratic autumn rains
pummel pecans to the ground.
The cracked black pieces,
like burnt biscuits,
tattoo the patio's canvas
with another season of nutmeat,
stains of sorrel and cinnabar
re-inking the gray concrete.
I think of her tarnished
thumb and forefinger—
too many joints,
too many years—
that precise color.

九月
司各特 · 威格曼

喜怒无常的秋雨
把山核桃打落在地。
裂开的黑碎片，
像烤焦的饼干，
用另一个季节的坚果肉
轻击庭院的篷布，
粟色与猩红的斑点
给灰色的混凝土重新上色。
我想起她黯然失色的
拇指和食指——
太多指节，
太多岁月——
恰到好处的颜色。

回故里

杨晓芸

步入中年的这个人
经历过悲伤和美好的这个人
走在风中，不再为风声所动
不再朝向深渊，投石子
不再期待
虚无之坻的回响
邻家的孩童急急拐过墙角
带走当年的明亮
无名的野花在身边摇曳
去年冬天的残枝
在它们的光芒中继续腐烂
直至无迹可寻

going back to the old neighborhood
Yang Xiaoyun

It would be better for one who enters middle age
one who goes through sorrow and happiness
walking in wind, not to be moved by the sound of the wind
not to throw stones into the abyss
not to expect
an echo from an island of emptiness
Neighborhood children quickly turn the corner of the wall
take away the brightness of those years
nameless wildflowers wave nearby
stalks left from the winter before
decay in the light
until no trace remains

October Revival in Texas
Scott Wiggerman

Swaying like a gospel choir,
their robes outstretched,
leaves swish overhead,
lifting spirits unseen for months
with sounds of celebration.

All that heat and humidity
swept away in soulful swoops,
long fanfares of gusts.
The dizzying roar of a norther
gives wings to gulps of pure joy.

The whoosh of the canopy—
like listening to a waterfall
from a grotto tucked behind it—
a sound so baptismal
you want to dive into the sky.

德克萨斯十月的复活

司各特·威格曼

像福音唱诗班一样摇摆，
他们的长袍展开，
叶子在头顶哗哗飘过，
用庆祝的声音
把数月不见的灵魂升上天空。

在深情的波动和悠长的
喇叭声似的风中，
那所有的热气和潮湿都被扫荡。
北风那令人眩晕的吼叫
给单纯快乐的吞咽插上翅膀。

天篷的嗖嗖声——
好像从瀑布
后面的洞里听到瀑布声——
一个洗礼的声音
让你想扑向天空。

梦见苹果和鱼的安

何小竹

我仍然没有说
大房屋里就一定有死亡的蘑菇
你不断地梦见苹果和鱼
就在这样的大房屋
你叫我害怕

屋后我写过的那黑森林
你从来就没去过
你总在重复那个梦境
你总在说
像真的一样

我们不会住很久了
我要把所有的门都加上锁
用草茎锁住鱼的嘴巴
直到天亮

你还会在那个雨季
用毯子蒙住头
倾听大房屋
那些腐烂的声音吗

dream of apples and fish
He Xiaozhu

I have not yet explained
that there must be a mushroom of death in a big house
you continually dream of apples and fish
in just such a big house
you scare me

the dark forest behind the house I wrote about
that you never set foot in
you always repeat that dream
you invariably say
it is all too real

we won't live here long
I'll have all the doors locked
and lock the fishmouth with a stalk
until daybreak

will you still in that rainy season
cover your head with a blanket
listening in the big house
to those rotting sounds

Afterward
Jerry Bradley

The dandelions bow
to the whirring blade
as I walk the mower

across the lawn
trying to beat
the approaching storm.

It is not fall
but soon will be –
in an hour perhaps.

So the lizard
seeks his shelter
under the chipped pot,

and frogs abandon
their dream of meeting
their lovers by the river.

Summer has been so hot
we all have had tropical thoughts:
chocolate-covered mangoes,

naked silhouettes in the shade,
crickets enjoying
their picnic in bed.

When the cold comes
and the distant mountains
whisper to the wind,

之后

杰里 · 布拉得雷

蒲公英弯向
旋转的刀片
在我推着割草机

走过草坪的时候
尽量赶在
将至的
暴风之前。

秋天尚未来到
但是很快将至——
说不准在一小时之内。

因此蜥蜴
在有缺口的桶下
寻找藏身之处。

青蛙放弃了
在河边
与情人幽会的美梦。

夏天太热了
我们都有过热带的想法：
涂满巧克力的芒果，

背阴处赤裸的剪影，
蟋蟀在床上
享受自己的野餐。

当寒冷到来
远山对风
喃喃低语，

the dim anarchy of change
will already have us, and like
the leaves we too will be defectors

until change too passes
and afterward
a small radio announces rain.

变化阴暗的无序
将已左右我们，如树叶
我们也将是逃兵

直到变化也过去
之后
小收音机预报有雨。

December
Aaron Rudolph

These days my life spins by, unfolding fast
under watch of gray clouds. Images speed
in flashes, in shrieks, in bits fragmented
to the rural towns of memory.

On the family trip, we drove in shifts.
Sleep made an eight-hour car trip feel
like half that, Midwestern cities blinking
in and out, gas stations hazy, the fog

of my eyes surrounding each town. My home,
birthplace: buildings of childhood, cold streets
worn, no snow in New Mexico and clouds
here, too, grow dark. Watch the washed-out colors

of winter: trees limping, skies shivering.
Somehow nostalgia paints a bright picture.

十二月

阿龙·鲁道夫

这些天我的生活疾驰而过，
在灰色云层的注目下迅速展开。
破碎的画面像闪电，嘶鸣，点点滴滴
飞驰到记忆的小城。

全家人外出旅行，我们轮流开车
睡眠使人感觉八小时的车程
缩短了一半，中西部城市时隐时现，
加油站模模糊糊，我眼里的雾气

笼罩着每一座城市。我的家，
出生地：童年的建筑，破旧寒冷的街道，
新墨西哥不下雪，在这儿也有云层
变暗。注视褪色的

冬天：树木蹒跚，天空哆嗦。
怀旧不知怎的绘成一幅亮丽的图画。

Burn
Nathan Brown

Oklahoma in July
is a marshmallow
in a bonfire;

a branding iron
on the fence;

a toad in the slow-
ly heated pot;

where Fahrenheit
screams until its eyes
turn red—

until the blood
rises in its mercurial veins.

燃烧

内森 · 布朗

七月的俄克拉荷马
是篝火中的
一颗果汁软糖；

一把架子上的
烙铁；

一只在慢慢加温的
锅里的蛤蟆；

水银温度计
发出尖叫
直到它的眼睛渐渐
变红

直到血液
在水银静脉里升腾。

坟墓

李森

从墓穴出来，抚摸着碑文
隔世的天书，不知道是耻辱还是光荣
被称作文字的花样，或者蛇蝎图案
罪恶的蝌蚪，一只蜘蛛，几滴露水
他转动了墓碑的方向，文字朝向墓穴
他不需要再进去，他出来了
他爱施舍的浆水和纸钱的灰烬

grave

Li Sen

out of the grave, fingering the inscription
heavenly book of another time: honor or dishonor, not known
drawings called words, or patterns of snakes and scorpions
evil tadpoles, a spider, a few drops of dew
he turned the tombstone, characters facing the pit
he does not need to go back in, he is out here
he loves the offerings: soup and ashes of paper money

贪婪

海男

关于贪婪，已经像绳子似的
开始捆绑住她的肉身
而在门槛外，那些长出了芽的土豆
使她的现实生活暂时失去了欢快

受其发芽土豆的牵引，她的手
控制不住汹涌，那一阵阵
缤纷的外在推动力，骤然间
已经把她副到了崖顶

而她的贪婪，仍然像一面从黑暗中
飘来的旗帜，削弱了她灵魂中的纯色
正沿着她荒凉的脊背在跳动
正沿着崖顶的荆棘在前行

greed

Hai Nan

with regard to greed, like rope it seems
to have commenced to bind her flesh
and beyond the threshold, the budding eyes of those potatoes
make her real life lose joy for a time

drawn by the budding eyes of the potatoes, her hands
cannot contain the turbulence, surge after surge
a profusion of powers from outside, abruptly
pushes her to the precipice

and her greed, like something on the sly coming out of darkness
a fluttering flag dissipates the pure color of her soul
pulses along the spine of her desolate back
along the thorny spine of the precipice

A Note of Thanks
Nathan Brown

I am terribly grateful to this morning's
low plains snow storm, a Vesuvian
display that floats in so softly, silently
to dust the flatlands with rapturous inactivity.

What command, with a single powdery hand,
to be able to halt all the silly motions
and illusory dreams of commerce.

My own kitchen table, windows onto whiteness,
a cup of tea, a bowl of oats and crunchy toast—
the stuff of an earthly heaven—a river
of love and letters onto these white pages.

道谢便条
内森 · 布朗

我非常感激今天早晨
平原上下的一场暴风雪，像维苏威火山
雪花飘飘那么温柔，那么沉静
用欣喜的休眠，去除平地的尘土。

什么样的指令，能用一只粉扑扑的手，
中止一切愚行和
虚无缥缈的商业梦。

透过白花花的窗户：在我的厨房餐桌上
摆着一杯茶，一碗燕麦粥，还有一块酥脆的烤面包——
人间天堂的俗物——爱河和字母
爱和文字流淌到空白的页面上。

故乡

李南

我常常羡慕他们，用手指指
遥远的方向
说，那是故乡

我没有故乡，梦中一马平川
绕过一棵棵树
独自来到蓝色大海的另一端

哦，青山作证
我也有沉重的乡愁
当世界沉沉睡去，我的故乡
在说也说不出的地方。

hometown

Li Nan

Often, often I admire them, point
To the far horizon
Say, that's hometown

I have no hometown, I dream a horse on an endless plain
Turn round tree by tree
Come alone to the far shore of the blue ocean

Oh, green mountain witnesses
Still, I am weighed down by yearning for hometown
As the world slept deep, deep, my hometown
A place I want to say but cannot speak

Dry Spell
David Meischen

Ants arrive in June and strip the oleanders.
Corn leaves curl and kernels shrivel, ruining
themselves with aflatoxin. Mornings, Elwood walks

the pasture, dew catching light in parched grass
and muddying dust on his boots. Hefting the heavy-
bladed grubbing hoe, he severs scrub mesquite trees

at the root. Others hold on, taproots deep enough
to suck up water and turn sunlight green. They wait,
sharp-edged, like prickly pear and spanish daggers.

When heat bends the Gulf-thick light, he walks
back to the house, hangs the grubbing hoe in its place
on the tractor shed wall, and sits beneath the hackberries,

cooling off. Queen's wreath whispers against
the rumble of trucks on the highway, tempered
by distance and sparrows. As a boy, Elwood watched

the highway unfold. They used mules to raise up
the roadbed, fed them Johnson-grass hay, seed
drifting along the Agua Dulce, runners burrowing
after rainfall, undaunted by dry spells. Inside,

he turns on the air at the dining window,
his house so quiet now, a stillness inside amber.
His sons and daughter smile from the walls,
the light that shines on unlined faces bright

干旱期

大卫·麦森

蚂蚁在六月到来，剥去了夹竹桃的皮。
玉米叶子变得卷曲，谷粒开始收缩枯萎，用
黄曲霉毒素毁掉了自己。早晨，埃尔伍德

在草原上散步，露珠在枯草间光亮耀眼
泥土灰尘沾满他的靴子。扛着沉重的
锄头，他开始了为那些矮小的牧豆树

除草。其它植物坚持挺立，根深深地扎进土里
吮吸水分，并把阳光转化成绿色。他们等待着，
锋利无比，像刺梨或凤尾兰。

当热浪弄弯墨西哥湾浓密的光线，他
走回家，把锄头挂回
拖拉机棚的墙上，之后走回家坐在朴树下

乘凉。蓝花藤喃喃私语。
抗拒高速公路上卡车的轰隆，距离
和麻雀从中调和。作为孩子，埃尔伍德看着

高速公路不断延伸。他们用骡子去垫高
路基，用约翰逊草喂它们，种子
顺着水沟漂流，大雨之后，
外勤人员挖掘地洞蓄水，不畏干旱。屋里，

他打开餐厅的窗户透透气，
他的房子现在如此安静，静如琥珀的内部。
他的儿女从墙上传来微笑，
光洁的脸上闪耀着光芒

as memory twenty years later. Everything
is where it should be, brass pheasants nesting
beside the couch, sewing machine in its corner
by the window seat, sunlight pooling there.

Elwood drives to town, plays dominoes
with men he's known so long their habits
have worn smooth at the edges, so many years
of the rough and jocular that grief can find no voice

among them. Back home he walks through heat
gone grey and mild beneath thickening shadows,
inside to his favorite chair. Beside him Valerie's
rocking chair sits empty. Elwood rests a hand

on its smooth polished arm, and pointing the remote,
clicks on television news. He will fall asleep here.
He will wake in the night to voices, flickering light.

明亮如二十年后的记忆。一切照旧
井井有条，雉鸡铜像在沙发旁
筑巢，缝纫机在靠窗座位旁的
角落里，那里洒满阳光。

埃尔伍德开车去镇上，与一个老相识
玩多米诺骨牌，他们的习惯在相处中
变得相似，多年的
艰苦和滑稽，悲伤却找不到声音。

回到家，走在渐浓渐密的树荫下面
变得灰白温和的热气，
坐在他最喜爱的椅子上。在他的身旁，维勒莉的
摇椅空着。埃尔伍德把手搭在

光滑闪亮的扶手上，按着遥控器，
调到电视新闻。他将在这里入睡。
也将在夜里从声音和摇曳的光亮中醒来。

Beyond the Entropy of Gophers
Jerry Craven

In darkness they claw closer, teeth
and belly taking roots from careless weed,
from Russian thistle, and sometime in the night
they gnaw to the surface for wrinkling the earth in waves
of furrowed threat toward us. Will our fence
repel a rodent appetite for iris
bulbs, for jonquil and rosemary? We think
not in a grim contemplation of poison.

My evening mirror shows once dawn-rust
strands graying among wrinkles, eyes
held in sagging skin yet determined to see
beyond Time gnawing furrows
in threats of final darkness. I find much
comfort knowing you and I will never
try the futility of stitching or stretching of skin
or botox needles for fences futile against
dark furrows, the entropy of gophers.

I'll hold your hand, kiss your lips, walk
with you beneath sweetgum in pine-
tree air, plant with you fresh thyme,
new iris, try with you young tree roots
in moist earth and await the springing of blossoms
and figs, the summering of fruit into
autumn apples red and golden; I'll take
your hand that we may stand together and kneel
together in planting jonquils pure and rosemary,
that we may triumph with purple crocus defying
snow, with carnations bright in autumn sun.

地鼠的混沌之外
杰里·克莱文

在黑暗中它们爬近，牙齿
和胃消耗着杂草根，俄罗斯蓟，
在夜晚的某个时刻
它们啃到地表起皱
形成威胁我们的一波波皱折。我们的栅栏
能否抵抗地鼠对鸢尾茎、
长寿花和迷迭花的胃口？我们
丝毫没想到毒药。

傍晚照镜子我看到从前是黎明锈色的线
在皱纹中变灰，眼皮松弛
仍然决心对土拔鼠
视而不见。时间在最终的黑暗威胁中啃着皱纹
知道你我从不徒劳地试着缝补或拉伸皮肤
或给栅栏安装肉毒针进行无效的抵抗
黑暗的皱纹、地鼠的混沌，我感到轻松。

我要握你手，亲你唇，
在松香中和你漫步于枫香树下，
和你一起栽种新鲜的百里香，
新的鸢尾花，和你一起试着把幼树根放在
微潮的土里然后等待开花的春天和无花果，
从夏果结成金红色苹果的秋天；
我要握着你的手 我们就可以一起站着和跪着
栽种纯洁的长寿花和迷迭花，
我们就有蔑视白雪的藏红花，
在秋日的阳光下闪耀的康乃馨，
我们或许因此获胜。

声音和羽毛
李森

今天清晨，声音和羽毛
突然在蓝天中诞生
就在这个时候，惟一的一片白云
失去了混沌的童真，但没有下雨
就在这个时候
山顶上潮湿的雀窝开始颤抖
所有的小鸟一起鸣叫
所有白色的羽毛，都已经长齐
河谷中平静的流水，也开始闪亮
无论在白天还是星空下
事物模仿着事物，永无休止
这是窗外的一幕，平淡无奇
在远方闪现了瞬间
观察者茫然失措，恐惧万分

sounds and feathers
Li Sen

this morning, sounds and feathers
suddenly born in blue sky
born in this moment, a single sliver of white cloud
lost its chaotic innocence, but it was not raining
at this moment
damp bird nests on hilltops started to quiver
all the birds in chorus cried
all the white feathers, all grown long already
tranquil running water in the valley began to glisten
whether in the day or under the starry night
things imitated other things, endlessly
this was the scene outside the window, nothing strange
a distant flash in a twinkling
observer lost in the dark, full of fear

Red-tailed Hawk
James Hoggard

Its feathers roughed by the north wind,
the hawk stayed fast on its live oak perch,
then slowly, as if releasing its breath in its wings,
it rose, higher now, then planed away fast
from the leafless mott, and it wouldn't return
till talons and beak had been washed
in a hot splash-bath of blood

红尾鹰
詹姆斯·霍葛德

它的羽毛被北风吹得蓬乱不堪，
鹰牢牢地站在活着的橡树上，
然后慢慢地，如呼气一般张开翅膀
它直起身，现在更高，然后准备迅速飞离
那光秃秃的矮树丛，它不会回来
直到双爪和喙，
在一场血腥飞溅的热浴中被洗刷

鸟群的声音
海男

鸟群的声音好像变了
沿着乡间小路的竖杆和一朵玫瑰的形状
鸟群在读书的诗人空间飞
鸟群在慈善的沃土中飞
鸟群偶然死去时，并不是鸟群的衰老
鸟群的年龄特别短，只有人类的千分之一
在鸟群短暂的时光中，鸟群没有限制的
比树木和积雪更加快乐
鸟群会死在雪地，旷野或一个人的草帽上
不知不觉地死去，比风声更细谧
鸟群一只比一只少，后来就会来一群
颜色较浅的鸟，它们是一群小鸟

the flock's voice
Hai Nan

The flock's voice seems changed
flying by poles on rural roads and the shape of a rose
flocks fly in the space of poets reading
flocks fly over fertile fields
flocks die by chance not age
flocks live short lives, a very small fraction of a human life
in their brief time, flocks know no limits
they are happier than trees and heaps of snow
flocks will die in snow, in wilderness, on a person's straw hat
die unaware, weightless as wind
the flock is one bird one bird less, and then will come
another lighter flock, they are fledglings

蝴蝶是怎样变成标本的
海男

死亡在一只蝴蝶身上表现出一阵抽搐
一阵阵流动的、轻快的、响应死神号召的
抽搐、或者说旋律。之后，蝴蝶有了它自己的
监狱，只有在房间里，在镜框下面，每一只蝴蝶

才可能变成标本，每一只蝴蝶是在绚丽之后
慢慢的停止飞翔的，飞累了的蝴蝶
飞得晕头转向的蝴蝶，飞得越来越灿烂的蝴蝶
在深沉的蓝雾里迷失在自由之中的蝴蝶

只有在监狱的房间和镜框里面，只有在一本书中
才可能变成标本，只有在一次死亡之后的抽搐之中
才可能保存下来全部的灿烂，只有在蝴蝶的监狱之中
才可能向世人展现它们短暂的一生

how a butterfly becomes a specimen
Hai Nan

Death is embodied in the instant of a butterfly's twitch
a fleeting convulsion, fluid, responsive to death's voice
a twitch, a melody. After that each butterfly is in its own
prison, only in a chamber in a building can each butterfly

become a specimen. Each butterfly after beautiful flight
gradually stops flying worn out with flying, each butterfly
dazed and disoriented, more and more brilliant each butterfly
lost in deep blue mist of freedom each butterfly

alone in its cell only in a frame only in a book only
can it become a specimen, in a convulsion after death only
can its whole splendor be preserved, in the prison of butterflies only
can their fleeting lives be put on public display

鸟禽畜牲都好歌

李森

在我们的时代
有一首歌
歌词大意是：
啊，咿呀咿
秃鹫好
鹰隼好
大雁好
天鹅好
猫头鹰好
海鸥好
海鸭好
鹦鹉好
喜鹊好
麻雀好
黄鹂好
斑鸠好
鹌鹑好
鸡好
鸭好
狗好
牛好
马好
猪好
猫好
老鼠好
豺狼好
虎豹好
蚊子好
苍蝇好
灯蛾好
蟑螂好
蚂蚁好
毒蛇好

song for the good birds and beasts
Li Sen

in our age
there is one song
and it goes like this:
ah, yi ya yi
vulture good
falcon good
wild goose good
swan good
owl good
seagull good
eider good
parrot good
magpie good
sparrow good
oriole good
turtledove good
quail good
chicken good
duck good
cow good
pig good
cat good
mouse good
wolf and jackal good
tiger and leopard good
mosquito good
fly good
moth good
cockroach good
ant good
serpent good

排名不分先后
不管是否提到的
普同供养
大家都好
啊，咿呀咿

in no particular order
named or unnamed
all share the offerings
everyone good
ah, yi ya yi

Mockingbird
Larry Thomas

In our all too human hubris
we've stuck you with a specious name,
plain bird yet so fiercely territorial
you'll attack a diamondback,
stab its eyes with the dagger of your beak,
and leave it writhing in blindness

to a death by its own venom.
Is it not the other birds which,
stupefied by the virtuosity of your singing,
have stolen but a shred of your cadenza
and made it the sole song of their being?
We just couldn't handle the terrible ease

with which you and you alone
broke each day with a music
so plangent it overshadowed
the breathless pastels of dawn,
so plangent we had to name you
and in our human frailty named you wrong.

We had to rob you of your grand creative prowess
and claim it as our own,
as the only thing which lofted us
above the lesser animals,
so we named you mocker,
hoarding maker for our false, false selves.

水蒲苇莺

赖里·托马斯

出于人类的妄自尊大
我们给你取了个华而不实的名字，
不起眼的鸟儿却那么凶悍地维护领地
你会攻击菱纹背泥龟，
用剑一样的喙刺瞎它的眼睛
让它在黑暗中挣扎

直到它在愤懑中死去。
其它的鸟难道不是
被你精湛的歌技吓懵，
不过盗取你一小节华彩乐段
就把它作为平生惟一的歌曲？
我们无法应对这骇人的轻松自如

你和你自己驾轻就熟地
用音乐唱响每一天的开始
这音乐如此凄切，令绚烂的黎明
黯然失色，
如此动人，让我们不得不为你命名
并出于人类的意志薄弱给你错误的命名。

我们不得不夺取你出类拔萃的创造力
并声称它是我们自己的，
作为使我们高于
低级动物的惟一的东西，
于是我们称你为嘲弄者，
掩藏了我们虚假、虚假自我的制造者。

送一颗炮弹到喜玛拉雅山顶
何小竹

送一颗炮弹
到喜玛拉雅山顶
我为这个想法而彻夜不眠
就好象我已经登上了
喜玛拉雅山顶
亲自看见在冰块和雪山之间
我送去的炮弹
正闪闪发亮

shoot a bomb to the top of the Himalayas
He Xiaozhu

shoot a bomb
to the top of the Himalayas
with the idea I toss and turn all night
as if I'd already climbed
to the top of the Himalayas
an eye-witness amidst glaciers and snow mountains
to the bomb I shot
shimmering

玻璃的味道
海男

玻璃有味道的传说
是由一个女人的嘴传递出来的
她不停地使用玻璃
似乎这世上没有任何东西与玻璃比美

玻璃在她的身体中央
可以成为屏风、镜框、镜面
在阴湿和阳光普照的时刻
她似乎把身体从玻璃中抽了出来

仿佛她的身体从玻璃中长了出来
如果她被碰撞，成为碎片
她一定是满地的水晶色，这味道
使暗哑中的桑带失语了

the flavor of glass
Hai Nan

the legend that glass has flavor
comes from a woman's lips
she ceaselessly uses glass, as though
nothing in the world could compare with glass in beauty

glass in the center of her body
can become a screen, a frame, a mirror
in moments of damp and sunshine
she seems to draw her body out from glass

as if her body had grown out from glass
if struck she would shatter to pieces
she must be the crystal color all over the ground, this flavor
robbing her mute vocal cords of the power to speak

Before the Coming of the Crow
Jerry Craven

Upon the canyon rim
sun dying clouds flame
a moment into perfection, the crow
squats waiting upon a locust limb,
the owl awaits predatory night,
and killing beetles sleep beneath the bark
while air distills into rippled hush
from Catclaw Creek
springing below
a cliff holding earth in shadows dim
and sky a dazzling present before dark.
It's time to see the buttercup wild flower
on vines green beneath these flaming skies,
taste its perfume, brush petals to a cheek
in holding back final desert night.
Until the moment dies
to static darkness, eternally the same,
I'll look to buttercups, for time runs lean,
make moments into years
forgetful of the coming hour
of the beetle, owl, the locust crow, and lock
with stinging eyes
a small forever into this twilight flame.
I'll banish tears
with love of cinnabar skies,
of jade matrix in tumbling rock,
of goatgrass and willow whips green lush
from spring water and perfect evening light,
with seeing golden flakes flashing in the green
presence of buttercup vine and flower.

乌鸦来临之前

杰里·克莱文

在峡谷边缘之上空
太阳染得云彩似火
在一个完美的时刻，
乌鸦蹲着等待一只蝗虫肢，
猫头鹰等待着打猎的夜晚，
食肉的甲虫睡在树皮下
此时空气因下面涌动的
猫爪溪
而酿成了泛起涟漪的沉默
陡崖把地面放在暗淡的阴影里
天空在黑暗前面亮得晃眼。
现在正是看燃烧的天空下
绿藤蔓上开放的野毛茛花的时候，
品味它的芳香，用花瓣轻拂面庞
为了抵挡最终的沙漠之夜。
直到这一时刻逝去
进入静止的黑暗，恒常不变，
我要注意毛茛，因为时间缩短了
把时时刻刻拉伸成岁岁年年
忘却属于甲壳虫、猫头鹰、吃蝗虫的乌鸦来临的时间，
并且用刺眼钉住黄昏火焰的一小片永恒。
我要拭去因爱上火红的天空、
滚石上的玉质、
山羊草和柳条
而涌出的眼泪
泉水边的绿草和完美的黄昏之光，
此时看见金色的薄片闪耀在
毛茛花和绿藤之间。

漂亮的奴隶
海男

水壶上，蒸汽上升着，一年中的午夜
用水和蒸汽开始设计花布和疲惫后穿的衣服
鸟尖叫着，跑进门来，用声音唤它，袭击它
鸟群的目标是为了飞完天空
附近的田洼，一架古老的织布机
现在只用来织出老年人的服装
土豆的作用、稻谷的压力、水渠的长远利益
物质淹没物质，音乐却战胜了
老年的寂静。水流到身体下面
从首都到云南，我根据地理和轨道
用不可弥补的空虚让手臂凉下去
奴隶，奴隶，我饮水时看见一个漂亮的奴隶

a pretty slave
Hai Nan

Above the kettle, steam rises, midnight of the year
weave water and steam into bright fabric and clothes to wear after
                                                    tiring work
birds shriek, run indoors, call to it, tear at it
the goal of the birds is to finish with sky
on low-lying land nearby lies an ancient loom
used only to spin for the old now
use of potatoes, pressure of grain, channel for long-term interests
matter swamps matter, music vanquishes
the solitude of old age. Water flows under the surface
from the capital to Yunnan, I follow tracks and the lay of the land
cool my arms with irremediable emptiness
slave, slave, while drinking water I see a pretty slave

Spring in Palo Duro Canyon
Jerry Craven

Dancing between the darkness of dawn and twilight
I, caught in burning April,
praise early the stations of the spring:
a desert stream; a land crowned by thorny mesquite,
careless weed, buffalo grass, cottonwood
(blessing brown soil with chlorophyl);
that canyon rim, aflame and vermilion
with sacred intercession from an exploding sun
and all else that new-made time creates
with tumbling light blazing winter earth
into this greening genesis of summer –
this air, a sacred confusion of bee, bird, and pollen,
this water, spawning shadows, alive with light,
this earth, holy with thistles and sage.

帕罗杜若峡谷的春天
杰里 · 克莱文

在黎明和昏暗之间跳舞
我，深陷火热的四月里，
早早地赞美春天的篇章：
一条沙漠小溪；多刺的牧豆树覆盖着土地，
杂乱的草，水牛草和白杨树
（把叶绿素的祝福给了褐色的土地）
峡谷的边缘，燃烧着火焰和朱砂，
爆炸的太阳，带来神圣的和解
还有新的时间滋生，用跌落的阳光创造一切
把冬日的土地燃烧成夏日绿色的源泉——
这空气，是蜜蜂、鸟儿和花粉神圣的混杂，
这水，喷涌着阴影，随阳光而生，
这土地，因蓟草和鼠尾草而神圣。

躺在三天宽的歌喉上

唐丹鸿

这脑海在高涨
这些激素把我们埋了

雨滴，像小巧的银弹
在她的脑门上爆炸
鞋子，沿着寻常的道路
划向狂躁之海
她把潮湿的肉体暂时交给毛巾
为了终有一刻能去交给荒谬！

雨水在毛巾中越陷越深
脑海从颅内拍打我的激素仓
我决定闭门不出，但没有干什么
一些障碍在吻我
腺体燃放焰火以祝福：

祝你躺在三天宽的歌喉上
祝带翅的力
祝一团盲云，两平方自由
祝你煽动她就是修理我
……的窗子，朝向心灵的感染区 –
雨后，晚霞开始乱来
高楼反弹着天上的红血球
立交桥涂满了静脉的青色！

这是道理她都明白的三天
被阻滞的工作像警察那样叱责我
你挣了挣，又蜷下去了
问毛巾"怎样积极？" –
拖沓的……神经棺材，反而我活着

这脑海再次高涨
这些激素再次把我们埋了

100

lie down on a voice singing three days wide

Tang Danhong

this brain is surging
these hormones bury us

raindrops, like exquisite little silver bullets
explode at the door of her brain
shoes, along the usual road
row to the sea of rage
she temporarily surrenders her damp body to the towel
to surrender in the end to absurdity!

rain sinks deep into the towel
brains follow through a flap in the forehead into my
                                   hormone storehouse
I decide to stay indoors, but get nothing done
a few little obstructions are kissing me
my glands set off fireworks as a blessing:

wish you lie on a voice singing three days wide
wish you winged strength
wish you a dumpling of blind clouds, freedom two square
wish you move her to mend me
......windows, toward the sick soul –
after rain, sunset clouds start to fuck around
high-rises catapult the bloody balls of the sky
overpasses are scrawled full of green veins!

these three days are the reason she understands
work obstructed scolds me like a cop
you earn and earn, go down again
ask the towel "how to be energetic?" –
sluggish......mental coffins, I live instead

this brain surges a second time
these hormones bury us once more

Condensation Nuclei
Wendy Barker

Sea salt, pollen, and smoke.
Particles the air
needs to form a cloud.
A pebble in the palm.
Phrase dropped on a plate.
Your words I've collected
and lined up like bowls
of ash, or sand,
stared at, and wept.
Or like our lidded glass
containers: oats and wheat,
opalescent grains
we use to knead
our bread, yeasty
loaves with bits of walnut.
Rain, relief, the irritants
washed back to loam.
Saliva, the body's
juices that digest
grit between our teeth.

致密的核

温迪·巴克

海盐、花粉以及烟雾。
空气中的微粒
要形成一朵云。
手掌中的鹅卵石。
词组落在盘子上。
你的语词
我已收集好
并排列得
像灰或沙做的碗
凝视，哭泣。
也像那有盖子的
玻璃器皿：燕麦和小麦，
乳白色的
用来做面包的谷物，
带核桃碎粒的发酵的面包。
雨水，调剂品，刺激剂被
冲刷回沃土里。
唾液，人体的汁液
消化着牙缝间的沙粒。

打开诗篇

李南

打开诗篇, 秋天的牧草
回家。在巨大的夜空下
我走过冷和孤单, 同时经受着
普通人的俗事和天才的命运

我祈祷过, 让美的一切飞翔
让大平原呼吸起来
我努力做着, 永不绝望

风把大地吹遍
我忍受着饥饿, 把丰收盼望
哦, 打开吧, 快打开诗篇

它告诉你, 朴素的思想
像群星一样闪亮
它让你听听, 我煅打的声音
贫穷击不跨高傲的头颅。

break open psalms
Li Nan

break open psalms, in autumn graze
homeward. Under a vast night sky
I pass by cold and lonely, touch of suffering at the same time
fate mixes genius with ordinary people and common affairs

I prayed, let every beautiful thing fly
let great plains begin to breathe
I strive to touch, never lose hope

wind blows everywhere on earth
I endure hunger, look forward to a bumper crop
oh, break open, break open psalms soon

it tells you, simple thought
that shines like many stars
it lets you listen. My voice forged
poverty can not break my back.

Windmills
Sherry Craven

Later, after I left you,
I came back to the ranch
to get my things.
You followed me carrying a Coors, disguised
in the crinkled brown of a paper sack.
The yellow and warm air was clear,
filling up the day like a cup of hot tea,
snakes asleep, birds awake, we neither.
Mesquite barely fuzzing to lime green, and
Johnson grass thrusting itself into spring.
I reached for the turquoise bath towels, the red
canister set, the drinking glasses with windmills
on them. You said, "No." If you couldn't have me,
I couldn't have them.
So, I left again – if I didn't take away the things we shared,
I wasn't leaving altogether, like withdrawing all
but ten dollars from a bank account,
hoping to build up more later.
I pulled my car onto the caliche dirt road,
12 miles to the highway, to the world,
leaving you installed in front of the tv,
needing someone, something to blame.
Years later, though I know you have moved
away, to town, I still see you snagged in the armchair
your shirttail caught in the cushions,
and hear the soft clanking of the windmill
as it draws water from the ground,
to make things grow,
something we could never do.

风车

雪莉·克莱文

稍后，我离开了你，
我回到农场
取我的用品。
你跟着我，带着一瓶清啤，
隐藏在皱巴巴的棕色纸袋里，
一杯热腾腾的茶，装满了岁月，
黄色和温暖的空气洁净透明，
蛇睡觉，鸟醒着，我们半睡半醒。
牧豆树刚刚发出毛茸茸的绿色，
约翰逊草把自己挤进春天里。
我伸手去拿绿松石浴巾，红色
咖啡小罐，印有风车图案的
玻璃杯。你说："不"。如果你得不到我，
我就得不到它们。
于是，我又一次离开——如果我不带走我们分享过的物品，
我就没有完全离开，就像从银行帐户
提取全部存款，还留下十美元，
希望越攒越多。
我驱车上了砾石小路，
距离公路，距离世界十二英里，
丢下你，安坐在电视机前，
想要责备某人或是某物。
多年以后，虽然我知道你已经搬走，
到了镇上，我仍然看见你瘫坐在扶手椅上
衣摆压在坐垫下，
还听见风车轻柔的叮当声，
仿佛它正从地上汲水，
使生命成长，
而这个，我们从未做到。

我写下的都是卑微的事物

刘春

我写下的都是卑微的事物
青草，黄花，在黑夜里飞起的纸片
冬天的最后一滴雪……
我写下它们，表情平静，心中却无限感伤——
那一年，我写下"青草"
邻家的少女远嫁到了广东
我写下"黄花"
秋风送来楼上老妇人咳嗽的声音
而有人看到我笔下的纸片，就哭了
或许他想起了失散已久的亲人
或许他的命运比纸片更惯于漂泊
在这座小小的城市
我这个新闻单位卑微的小职员
干着最普通的工作
却见过太过注定要被忽略的事
比如今天，一个长得很像我父亲的老人
冲进我的办公室
起初他茫然四顾，然后开始哭泣
后来自然而然地跪了下去
他穿得太少了，同事赶紧去调高空调的温度
在那一瞬，我的眼睛被热风击中
冬天最后的那一滴雪
就从眼角流淌出来

all I write about are insignificant things
Liu Chun

all I write about are insignificant things
grass, a yellow flower, a night flying scrap of paper
last flake of winter snow …
I write them down, expression tranquil, but not without
boundless sorrow in my heart——
one year I write "grass"
a young neighbor girl marries in Guangdong
I write "yellow flower"
Autumn wind sweeps the sound of an old woman's cough upstairs
and there are people who read the paper under my pen, then weep
perhaps another remembers family long lost
perhaps his fate is accustomed to a more drifting paper
in this little town
in my insignificant little press office
I work the most ordinary job
destined to witness too much to be entirely overlooked
today, for example, someone who looks very much like my
                                                elderly father
storms into my office
at first he looks lost, then he bursts into tears
afterward involuntarily goes to his knees
he must wear too little, a coworker hastens to adjust the
                                               air conditioner
that one wink, a warm wind strikes my eye
last flake of winter snow
at once tears come to my eyes

a nightingale risks
Natasha Marin

a lone
long feather wondering
at the sun.

He prefers to peel
his voice away
to the clumsy
tune of high tide,

but nagged at the blood
folding at his ear,
he bowed instead.

Why spend hours
pulling your skin about
freedom
when you are trapped
in "a someone"-suit?

I'm no expert
but I know a rouse
when I hear
the cellophane crackle
of his step.

He's no cowboy, but
the heavy-heeled metallic
wince in his gait
is distinctly black
and soft
like sifted soot.

夜莺冒险

娜塔莎·马林

一片孤伶伶的
修长的羽毛
诧异于太阳。

他情愿剥开
自己的嗓音
直达高潮处
那笨拙的曲调,

埋怨血统
掩上耳朵,
勉强鞠躬。

当你身陷
"某某"衣服里
为何还要费时
欺骗你的皮肤
去追求什么自由?

我不是专家
但当我听到
他脚步里
包装纸的噼啪声
我恍然大悟。

他不是牛仔,但
鞋跟沉重,金属
在他的步履中
生出漆黑
柔软
像筛过的烟灰。

这一天

吉木狼格

这一天就这样，不管我在哪里
睡一觉醒来，就是这一天了

这一天总会到来
我的一生有很多这一天

我等待着这一天
没有这一天就没有我

我又将浪费这一天
我认为我应该伤感

即使活一百岁
也就三万多天

一天很短，三万多个一天
也很短，短到只有一百年

我喜欢这一天
我喜欢不知道会发生什么事情

这一天爱情近在咫尺
又远在天边

这一天许多程序要完成
这一天我多半要喝酒

this day
Jimu Langge

this day is like this, no matter where I
wake from sleep, this day is

this day will eventually come
in my life there are many days like this day

I wait on this day
without this day there is no I

I'll probably waste this day
I admit I should lament

even if one lived to be a hundred
there would be only thirty thousand such days

one day is awfully short, thirty thousand one days
are awfully short too, as short as a hundred years

I like this day
I like not knowing what's going to happen

on this day love is near
and also far as the horizon

on this day many routines to follow
on this day I mostly want a drink

Holy is a fragile thing...
Sherry Craven

Holy is a fragile thing,
a crimson cardinal wing, brilliant,
clinging to a branch building
a nest for sacred and safe living.
I can almost see holy
as it hovers above the ground
feathery and hushed, motes
of hope sailing on the sun-air
of morning, or floating over my bed
to warm the covers on my
not-so-eager body.

Holy is invisible everywhere,
a celluloid negative of the day,
capturing, holding sacred the moments,
like my three year-old granddaughter
when she wants something, a cookie,
a gift from Wal Mart, anything,
I open my eyes wide to see,
strain against daily living, paying bills,
dirty laundry, a sink full of dishes,
a friend whose troubles overload
the telephone line.

I push my heart against my chest
to see holy; I know it is there
in faint notes of a wind chime,
a driver who lets you enter a line
of heavy traffic, the spouse who
forgives when you are unkind,
the waiter who remembers you
wanted no ice in your water.
Holy dances across a sunny road,
rises up with morning fog, pushes its head
through the garden soil, glazes the moon silver.

神圣是个纤弱的东西……

雪莉·克莱文

神圣是个纤弱的东西，
一只鲜红色的翅膀，光彩熠熠，
粘连在一幢边楼上
神圣和安全的生活巢穴。
我几乎看到了神圣
当它在大地上盘旋
轻如羽毛而无声无响，微小的
希望在早晨阳光灿烂的空气里
飘动，或在我的床上方漂浮
温暖着我的被子
和我不那么热切的身体。

神圣无处可见，
记录一天生活的电影胶片，
捕捉并保留着神圣的瞬间，就像我三岁的孙女
当她想要什么的时候，一块曲奇，
一件从沃尔玛买回的礼物，任何东西，
我睁大眼睛去看，
日常生活的压力，买单，
脏衣服，满水池的碗碟，
麻烦多得使电话线超负荷的
朋友。

我的手紧贴胸腔
去感觉神圣；我知道它就在那儿
在风铃微弱的声音里，
交通拥堵时让你先行的
司机，当你发火时
对你包容的爱人，
记得你的水里不加冰的服务生。
神圣轻舞着穿过阳光明媚的道路，
随着晨雾上升，从花园的泥土里
探出头来，给月亮镶上银光。

Holy isn't fancy or
even unfathomable.

Holy is right here if I can
just remember to catch the scarlet wing of
the cardinal glimmering in the tree outside
the kitchen window while
I pour my morning cup of coffee.
If I can just remember.
If I can just remember.

神圣并非幻想
甚或高深莫测

神圣就在这里，如果我能
在早晨倒咖啡的时候
记得去抓住厨房窗外
在树上闪光的
鲜红的翅膀。
如果我能记得。
如果我能记得。

我就将爱上五月

黄芳

四月就将带着内心的苦离开。
我就将爱上五月。

路上大雾宽阔，
河边桃花盛开。
低飞的鸟群，
羽翅忧伤又沉重。
——我手腕上的伤，
鲜艳又纯洁。

四月的传奇就将被大雾覆盖。
我就将爱上五月。

I will fall in love with May
Huang Fang

April's about to leave my heart bitter.
I will fall in love with May.

On the way a great fog,
riverside peach blossoms blooming.
A flock of birds flies low,
with grievous and heavy wings.
——the wound in my wrist,
bright and pure.

April romance will be shrouded in mist.
I will fall in love with May.

花儿
唐丹鸿

我的花儿不会向你要肥料
只有鲜血顺着花茎滴下来

我的花儿正在枯萎
她心甘情愿地快活地枯萎

当鲜血流出花儿滴给你

我的花儿是你的母亲
你是你的花儿的母亲
你的花儿也是母亲

bloom
Tang Danhong

my bloom won't ask you for fertilizer
only bright blood dripping down the stem

my bloom withers
she willingly merrily withers

when bright blood drips into the bloom for you

of you my bloom is mother
of your bloom you are mother
and your bloom too is mother

遥寄江南

李南

妹妹，我不曾见过你的蜂箱
山高水远
路过的电影院，播放着欧美大片
这和北方是一样的。

江水流淌，它们诉说着几千年的别离
你诗中的石竹花独自开了

答应我，你不许在暮色中唱起哀歌
不许把红色的事物看成血。
答应我，我们要把美德在大地上传播
还要在这个世界再活一辈子。

妹妹，我们都没有读到过死亡诏书
我们想像不出天堂和人间
究竟有什么不一样。

mail from the southern reaches of the Yangtze
Li Nan

Little sister, I have not yet seen your beehive.
The mountain is high, the river long.
The movie theater I pass, playing European and American films,
this is the same as the North.

Rivers, weep tales of a thousand year separation.
In your poems, China Pink flowers blossom.

Promise me, you will not sing a sad song at twilight.
Don't mix things red with blood.
Promise me, we will spread virtue on the earth,
live one more life in this world.

Little sister, we have not yet read the edict of death.
We cannot imagine heaven in the human world.
They are, after all, not at all the same.

Drink Water
Patricia Goodrich

If this were a heart transplant, the doctor would say my body's rejecting it. Foreign environment whose names even are foreign *arroyo – chamisa.* Air thinned blue, the sky, my blood oxygen sucked out of it. All curves – the foothills, the buildings, the walls. The walls can't keep the sky out.

Are my shoulders rounding, my back humping to become landscape? I would be absorbed except the ground is too arid to accept me. I'd imagined a parched, cracked earth, patterned like the geography on the back of my hands. But to crack, there must have first been water. Water is missing here.

Drink lots of water. Powdered dirt that won't even take the track of bobcat on the arroyo slope. Like herbs hanging upside down, the earth has lost its color – what once was ochre, now nondescript. *Drink water.*

Why does the sky without oxygen grow bluer at this altitude and the earth without water lose its red? My heart pumps, my body a bridge between earth and sky.

饮水
帕特丽夏·古德里奇

如果这是一颗移植的心，医生会说我的身体在排斥着它。在异国他乡，连名字都是陌生的 arroyo - chamisa。空气变成稀薄的蓝，天空，我的血液从中吸吮氧份所有的曲线——那些山丘，那些楼房，那些墙。墙壁无法将天空挡在外边。

是我的肩膀在蜷缩，背脊在隆起，从而变成风景吗？我将会被吸收，只不过土地太干燥，无法将我接纳。我想象过一个被烘烤的、裂开的大地，仿佛我手背上的地形。但要裂开，必须先有水。这里缺水。

饮很多的水。连粉尘也不会追逐野猫在旱谷斜坡上留下的足迹。像倒挂着的药草，大地失去了它的颜色——曾是赭色的，现在难以名状。饮水。

在这个海拔无氧的天空何以变得更蓝？无水的大地何以失去了它的赭红？我的心抽动我的身体，一座天地间的桥梁。

私秘中的露台
海男

早晨十点钟，她站在露台上晾衣
暖洋洋的光线使她的手指
像弓弦般温柔。她伸出手去
抚摸了衣角上那些皱褶中的泡沫

下午五点半钟，她在露台上收衣
泡沫们已经失去了踪迹
皱褶们已经丧失了力量
洗干净的衣服在她胸前搅紧了一阵香味

午夜十二点，她在露台上发呆
流星从她胸前滑过
移开了一阵阵阴郁中的时间
犹如一只暗盒再一次合拢

private balcony
Hai Nan

at ten in the morning, she's on the balcony drying clothes
sunlight pleasantly warm makes her fingers
supple as bowstrings. she extends her hand
caresses the foam in the wrinkles of the clothes

at half past five, she's on the balcony gathering clothes
every trace of foam is gone
the wrinkles have relaxed
clean clothes clutch fragrance in her bosom

at midnight, she's on the balcony lost in a trance
a meteor streaks across her bosom
takes time in fits of gloom
like a black box snapping closed again

———

在广阔的世界上
李南

在广阔的世界上，我想
万物是一致的。
禽兽、树林、沉寂的旷野
要呼吸，要变化 在悄悄之中发生……
星宿有它的缄默，岩石有自己的悲伤
要倾诉，要流泪
还要披上时空的风霜。

in the wide world
Li Nan

In the wide world, I think to myself
all beings are one.
Birds and beasts, forests, still wilderness
want to breathe, want to change
inside quietly quietly...
Silent star, sorrowing stone
want to speak, want to weep,
still want to scatter frost on empty wind.

Grace Strokes
Kenneth Hada

There are those bright cloudless mornings
that overshadow your mood,
create within your confusion a respite
where breath and hope coexist
the way a canoe glides through silent water
at sunrise, my rowing my attempts at faith,
striking the oar into water,
breaking the glass surface that holds
so much promise but keeps it
a lifetime away, the transparent wall
between me and happiness.

I push the oar deeper below the surface,
past brokenness and feel energy swirl,
transfer upward to my forearms
through synapses into shoulder,
into heart, into brain – and the act triggers
memories with every stroke –
and I cringe in pain at how it is that I
have come to this place and time of losing,
but I also know that each stroke propels me
further from that pain and closer
to tomorrow where clouds and sunshine
merge into bliss, and memories,
like oars in the mysterious water,
grace me past the pain,
past fearful claims of a future.

优雅地划桨

肯尼斯·哈达

那些晴朗无云的早晨
笼罩着心情
在迷茫中创造
呼吸与期冀同在的间歇
仿佛小舟
划过日出时寂静的水面
我摇桨
尝试着去信仰，击桨入水
敲碎如镜的水面——它负载着
太多的承诺，却又用一生一世
来隔离，透明的墙隔断幸福与我。

我把桨深深插入水面之下，
透过这破碎
感受漩涡的力量传向手臂
透过肌腱传到肩膀
浸入心灵和脑海
每一个划桨的动作唤起回忆——
而我蜷缩于痛苦之中，不知
为何沦落到这失意的地点和时刻
但我也知道，每一次划动都把我推离痛苦
推向明天那里的云彩和阳光
融合成狂喜和回忆，像桨
在神秘的水域，推送我
穿越痛苦，越过未来
可怖的索取。

疼

李南

今早起来，就看见孩子们在玩耍
奔跑在立秋后的大地上
小小的身子藏在大树的后面。

他们唱着不连贯的谣曲，秋天的风
把歌声，一波一波送来
使人们听到了天堂的赞美诗

所以他们叫孩子。穿了鲜艳的小衣衫
说笑着，争论着些简单的问题
他们单薄单薄的生命，被风吹起

他们是那样易折，身不由己地
随风而去。也是那样的幸运
盲目而结实地生长着。

哦，他们当中也一定有神的孩子
在美丽的山峰之间，在欢乐之间
悄悄地穿行

不，他们一定都是神的孩子
是上天赐给平民的珍宝
又是我们苍茫的心中，久久的疼。

it hurts
Li Nan

When I rise this morning, I see children playing,
running on fields of early Autumn,
hiding tiny bodies behind big trees.

They sing a broken string of familiar songs, borne on
Autumn wind, wave after wave.
People turn to listen to their heavenly anthems.

This is why they are called children. Wearing colorful clothes,
chattering and laughing, arguing over little things,
their thin thin lives flutter off on rising wind.

They change so easily, snap. Unable to control their own life,
gone with the wind. But they are lucky too,
blindly growing rooted to earth.

Oh, they must be children of God
among beautiful hills, in happiness
quietly quietly passing.

No, they must all be God's children,
treasures for common folk,
endless pain in our boundless hearts.

Mirage
David Meischen

Once when I ran a red light on Main Street
George threw himself to the floorboard
screaming. I stuck my head out the window
and barked at the empty streetscape.
Kingsville was flat and bright under spring sun,
so quiet with looming summer our noises never

lasted. Weekends we drove out to Padre Island.
waded naked into the Gulf at midnight,
salt spray against our lips, waves cresting
and ebbing—the tidal surge and pull of sea
against sand. And the full moon, its wet glimmer
whispering of something we wanted.

Sunday afternoons we drove back to Kingsville.
Prickly pear blossoms clustered bright
as jungle parrots against cactus leaves
thick with springtime juices, coastal grasses
shimmering green against the flat backdrop of sky.
And the quiet town ahead, dusty grid-work
of families home from church, and somewhere
on Main Street, our traffic light, turning red.

海市蜃楼

大卫·麦森

我曾在干道上闯红灯
乔治迅速卧倒，并大声尖叫
我从窗户探出头去对着空空的街景嚎叫。
在春天的阳光下，京斯威尔显得是那样平坦和明亮
静悄悄地，随着隐隐约约的夏日，我们的噪音不再

持续。周末我们驱车到帕德雷岛
在午夜我们赤身裸体走入墨西哥湾
带着咸味的飞沫击打着嘴唇，波浪高低起伏
——潮水拍打着细沙。
而空中的满月温润的微光
似乎在喃喃讲述我们想知道的事情。

星期日下午我开车回到京斯威尔
多刺的梨木花团锦簇，鲜艳夺目
就好像丛林中的鹦鹉与仙人掌的叶子相映成趣
春天的梨木花厚实而丰润
就好像海岸边泛绿的香草长在平滑的天幕上
前方安静的小城，一个个从教堂回家的家庭
星罗棋布，风尘仆仆
在主街的某个地方，交通指示灯变红了。

等待
冉仲景

梦里磨牙，醒来磨刀
我所等待的敌人迟迟没有到来

他的名字，压迫着我的心脏
我的脉搏因此紊乱

他疾行的脚步，踩熄了
我在原野里点亮的九十九盏马灯

我的牙掉了，我的刀钝了
天，渐渐渐渐就黑了

waiting
Ran Zhongjing

asleep I grind my teeth, awake I grind my sword
I am waiting for an enemy who has not yet come

his name oppresses my heart
my pulse races

his swift steps stamp out
ninety-nine lanterns I kindled on the plain

my teeth fall out, my sword dulls
little by little sky darkens

那些花
杨晓芸

那些花将好看的倒影投到水面
碎裂，起伏
空白的水
有了生动的内容
转而零落，消匿，更深刻地投入
水之心呵我的心
锲而不舍的花儿
怀着不禁的情欲
明年三月准时又开放

those flowers
Yang Xiaoyun

those flowers mirrored on water's surface
fall apart, ripple
fill blank water
with lively content
crumble, fade, cut deeper into
water's heart, my heart
resolute flowers
with unyielding desire
blossom again on time come March

The Acuña Brothers Look North, 1952
Aaron Rudolph

Weeks away from his fourth child,
no one is hiring carpenters. Julio's hands,
and his brother's, need fresh wood to pulse
in them, to feed them. Julio rivers his finger
north and south on a map ending in Montana,
three mountainous states away. Juan rereads
their cousin's letter from Butte. "They are hiring
Mexicans," he writes. "Plenty of work."

As boys, the brothers pledged to never leave
New Mexico. They chased the currents
in the Río Bravo, caught as many fish bare-
handed as they did with poles. They foot-raced
the Picuris Reservation boys and when they lost,
paid their debts in wooden coyotes and eagles,
hand-carved animals running or gliding forward.

阿库纳弟兄看北方，1952 年

阿龙·鲁道夫

在他第四个孩子出生几周后，
没有人雇木工。胡里奥的手，
以及他兄弟的手，需要新鲜的木头在其中跳动，
喂它们。胡里奥的手指
在地图上从北到南游走，停在蒙大拿，
三座山城之外。胡安重读
他们的表亲从比特寄来的信。"他们要雇
墨西哥人，"他写道。"有很多活儿"。

还是男孩的时候，弟兄们就发誓决不离开
新墨西哥。他们在布拉沃河急流中捕鱼，
空手抓到的鱼和用鱼竿钓到的一样多
他们和皮古立人保留地的男孩赛跑，
如果他们输了，就要给对方木制的狼和鹰，
手工雕刻的，正在奔跑或滑行的动物。

五十年代的语言
翟永明

生于五十年代 我们说的
就是这种语言
如今 它们变成段子
在晚宴上 被一道一道地
端了上来

那些红旗、传单
暴戾的形象 那些
双手紧扣的皮带
和嗜血的口号 已僵硬倒下
那些施虐受虐的对象
他们不再回来
而整整一代的爱情 已被阉割
也不再回来

生于五十年代 但
我们已不再说那些语言
正如我们也不再说 "爱"
所有的发声、词组、和语气
都在席间跳跃着发黄
他们都不懂 他们年轻的发丝
在阳光下斑斓 象香皂泡
漂浮在我的身边
他们的脑袋一律低垂着
他们的姆指比其它手指繁忙
短信息 QQ
还有一种象形字母:
生于五十年代
我们也必须学会 在天上飞奔的语言

1950s language
Zhai Yongming

born in the 1950s   we spoke
this kind of language
nowadays   they've become passages
served   at dinner parties
one after another

those red flags, leaflets
tyrannical images   those
tightly fastened belts
those blood-thirsty slogans   now fallen and stiff
those sadomasochistic objects
would never come back while
the love of the whole generation   castrated
will likewise never come back

born in the 1950s   yet
we no longer speak that language
just like we no longer say "love"
every vocalization, phrase, intonation
leaps yellow between banquets
they no longer understand   their youthful hair
glistens brightly in the sun   like soap bubbles
afloat around me
their heads invariably hang low
their thumbs are busier than other fingers
with SMS QQ
and an ideographic language as well:
born in the 1950s
we must master   these languages flitting in the sky

所有那些失落的字词
只在个别时候活过来
它们象撒帐时落下的葡萄、枸杞和大枣
落在了我们的床第之间
当我喃喃自语 一字一字地说出
我的男友听懂了 它们
因此变得腥红如血

all those words lost
rarely come back alive
like fruits of Chinese wolfberry, grapes and big Chinese dates
they fall onto the bed when the mosquito nets are spread
when I mutter to myself   one word after another
my boyfriend gets them   so they
must turn red as blood

Gift

Alysa Hayes

We'd made our way up
the stone steps along the falls.
Evening mist slicked back
mountains to a slow blooming blur.
The rock path shimmered at our ankles,
but the boy before us wasn't aware
of when our hands unclasped.
He only wanted the money,
a few pesos for the story.
This rock was once a man,
blessed by the gods, he said. See,
this cleft is his thin mouth opening
when he found out he wasn't dying
nor being forgotten. He fell
in horror. We'd listened
in darkness, bird rumor, and blue leaves,
chilled by the long hiss on our backs.
The falls—then the boy—far off
echoes downsloped. You
leaned in close, then turned
too quickly, reaching out to be caught,
finally looking at me
like I was someone you needed.

礼物

艾莉莎·海斯

我们艰难地往上走，沿着
瀑布旁的石阶向上攀爬。
暮霭缭绕的群山
滑回渐渐浓重的迷蒙中。
岩石小径在我们的脚踝处闪着微光，
可当我们松开紧握的手时
我们前面的男孩儿却浑然不觉。
他只想要钱，
为他讲的故事讨几个比索。
这块石头原来是个男子，
得到了神佑，他说。瞧，
这个裂缝，是他张开的嘴巴
当他发现他既没有死
也没有被遗忘的时候
他陷入了
恐惧之中。我们在黑暗中
聆听，鸟的传言，蓝色的叶子，
身后长长的嘶嘶声，不寒而栗。
瀑布——接着是那男孩——远远地
回声滑下山坡。你
在我身旁侧身，随后飞快地
转身，伸出手想要被握住，
最后注视着我
仿佛我是你需要的人。

阿根廷蚂蚁

吉木狼格

它们爬上船挺进欧洲
登陆后
以家族的名义迅速壮大
它们不断进攻
逐一消灭欧洲的蚂蚁
从而占领欧洲
它们继续乘船挺进别的地方
比如澳大利亚
不管在哪里
它们都能识别亲缘关系
并联合起来发动进攻
你可以轻易地捏死一只
阿根廷蚂蚁
但你无法将它们全部捏死
它们在洞穴生活
还是在野外作战
你得承认
世界不光是我们的
也是阿根廷蚂蚁的

Argentine ants
Jimu Langge

they boarded ships to march on Europe
after landing
they quickly expanded in the name of the clan
they incessantly attacked
and wiped out European ants one by one
thus occupying Europe
they continued their march elsewhere by ship
for instance Australia
wherever they were
they recognized family ties
and made joint attack
with your fingertips you can easily pinch one
Argentine ant dead
but you can't kill them all
they live in caves
and also fight in the field
you have to admit
that the world is not just ours
but also Argentine ants'

Midsummer Farewell
Jerry Craven

Golden in July sun, her black hair floating,
she walked the twisted juniper,
the saber lily, mesquite
and grassy paths of Palo Duro Park,
living the canyon night
beneath a jagged cottonwood's thrust into damp
blackness green amid
neon specks and oval moon floating
in leaves, in owl song
low along the palisading echo,
in the splash of desert waters where all
deny the zodiacal crab
within her veins.

Her black hair floating, her skin golden in blue
cotton she walked cement
and pavement to floors squared
in linoleum gray and stairs of false granite
with halls awash in neon
flicker to bring her valediction to us
and summer, her blue eyes
gray for the twisted juniper and cottonwood life,
stars, moon and feathered
lilies left beyond these Sheetrock
and painted walls,
beyond blinded eyes
and cancerous claws of darkness.

仲夏之别

杰里·克莱文

在七月的阳光里，她的黑发飘扬，金光闪闪，
她走过弯曲的杜松、
鸢尾、牧豆树间
还有帕罗多若公园绿草茵茵的小路上，
在参差不齐的棉树丛刺入的潮湿
黑暗的绿色下面，周围
是萤火虫和叶间漂浮的月亮，
伴随着猫头鹰的歌唱和岩壁上低沉的回音，
在飞溅的沙漠之水里
在那里一切都否定她静脉中
黄道蟹。

她的黑发飘扬，她的皮肤在蓝色的棉花中
泛着金光，她走过水泥和石头路
来到灰得像漆布的方形地面
假花岗岩台阶，到处红光闪烁的大厅
带着她向我们和夏天辞别的诗句，
她蓝色的眼睛变成灰色 为了弯曲的杜松
和棉树的生命，
星星、月亮和毛百合
被留在这些石灰胶板、
粉刷过的墙之外，
在瞎了的眼睛和恶性肿瘤般的黑夜爪子之外

押韵是有瘾的

吉木狼格

幸好我只吸烟
不押韵
我决不说
一二三四五
上山打老虎
这一刀切下来的韵太过分了
不论对六还是对七
老虎更惨，与五配对
老虎成了老五
我想让我的语言
像流水一样
而水是不押韵的
只管乱流、乱响
有些伙计
他们在音上加以注意
却忍不住到意上去玩
上句是东
下句必然是西
他们不懂他妈的自由
是多么的自由
押韵像他们打着的一把伞
而自由
连天空也不要

rhyming is addictive
Jimu Langge

fortunately I just smoke
not rhyme
I'll never say
one two three four five
go up to the mountain to hunt the tiger alive
this neatly trimmed rhyme goes too far
no matter if it matches with six or seven
the tiger alive is even more pitiful, rhyming with five
the tiger becomes the number five
I want to let my language flow
like running water
but water doesn't rhyme
it runs wild and rattles instead
some fellows
heed sound
yet cannot help playing with sense
if the first line orients east
the next line surely goes west
they don't know how free
damned freedom is
rhyming is like the umbrella they hold
whereas freedom
is unwanted even by sky

Blue in the Middle of a Corn Field
Alysa Hayes

These stalks don't wave like corn.
I never seen a sight more sorry
than harvest time come to an empty barn.
We had two horses, Grace and Nell,
shot by Mr. Daniels down by the river's
bend. This morning I thought bout the bodies
pushed out to water, the gray hide slicked back
on the flanks, ears flying limp and wet.
Wonder if they floated all the way down
to the sea: two horses in the ocean,
legs tumbled like stray feathers
by deep-water currents, long heads and hair
drifting among the big fish. Somewhere,
someone's gonna eat good tonight.

玉米地里的忧伤
艾莉莎·海斯

这些秆子不似玉米般起伏。
我从未见过比丰收时节
空空如也的粮仓更遗憾的场景。
我们本来有两匹马，葛瑞斯和内尔，
被丹尼尔先生击中倒在了河流的
弯道位置。今天上午我曾想到它们的尸体
被推到水里，灰白的鬃毛光滑地
掩在胁下，漂浮着的耳朵耷拉而潮湿。
不知它们是否沿河一路漂到了
大海：两匹马在海里，
腿晃动着，就像深海激流旁
飘零的羽毛，长长的头和鬃毛
在鱼群里漂动。今晚，某处，
某人将大饱口福。

不是一头牛，而是一群牛
何小竹

那天的确也是这样
先是一个农民牵来一头牛
让我们拍照
后来别的农民听说了
也把他们的牛从牛圈里牵出来
牵到雪地上
让我们拍照
副县长说，够了，够了
别牵来了
记者们没有胶卷了
但农民们还是把所有的牛都牵了出来
他们都想给自家的牛
照一张像

not one head of cattle, but a herd of cattle
He Xiaozhu

the other day really it was like this
first a farmer pulled a head of cattle
to let us take pictures
later other farmers got wind
and then pulled their cattle out of the pen
onto the snowfield
to let us take pictures
deputy magistrate said, enough, enough
don't pull more
the reporters have no more film
but the farmers still pulled all their cattle
because they all wanted their own cattle
to have headshots

A Single Sheep, One Cow
Jerry Bradley

in a day you can reach new worlds
on strings of bright beads, roads
stretching behind the horizon's neck
and glimpse game birds in shivery quadrilles
hives of bees, memorials to pigs and forgotten breeds
dogs and parcels of geese stammering

I hunt for you in the alphabet
each letter burdened with sound
it is an abecedarian game we play
what does the sheep say? the cow?
as we pass familiar shapes
our recognition forever pointing
us toward words
until we think of death

alone in our species
and terrified
we wonder when the road turned?
how? where are you?
and what does your heart say now?

一只绵羊，一头牛

杰里·布拉得雷

一天之内你能到达新世界
在鲜亮的珠链上，公路
在地平线的脖子背后延伸
瞥见颤栗方阵中的猎鸟
蜂箱、猪和被遗忘的幼仔，
狗和一群结结巴巴的鹅。

我在字母表里搜寻你
每个字母都负担着声音
它是我们玩的字母游戏
绵羊说什么？牛呢？
当我们经过熟悉的形状
我们的识辨力永远
把我们引向单词
直到我们念及死亡

独处于人类之中
心怀恐惧
我们不知道路何时拐弯？
怎么转弯？你在哪儿？
而你的心现在又说着什么？

昆明的玫瑰

李森

昆明的玫瑰
跟白菜一样便宜
这样便宜的花儿
不能隐喻爱情
所以，在昆明
爱情与玫瑰无关
只有运输到北京
我们的玫瑰才有意义
在情人节的黄昏
昆明的玫瑰
让北京情人的欲望潮湿了
即使突然来了沙尘暴
情人们的欲火
也能烧红天空
仅仅一个晚上
我们的玫瑰
就在祖国的首都
虚构了千千万万颗红心
把成群结队的少女
改造成了婆娘

Kunming roses
Li Sen

Kunming roses
cheap as cabbage.
flowers so cheap
cannot be a metaphor of love
so, in Kunming
love has nothing to do with roses
only when transported to Beijing
do our roses signify
in the evening of Valentine's Day
Kunming roses
invite damp desire of Beijing lovers
even if a sudden sandstorm comes
the fire of lovers' desire
will burn the sky red
in a single evening
our roses
in the capital of our motherland
take in millions and millions of red hearts
a mass of young girls
reformed to old wives

The Last Laugh
Alan Berecka

Armed with my Daisy Winchester
filled with BBs, I left the house
with a friend from the neighborhood—
preteens on the prowl looking
for something to kill. We went down
to the Nine Mile Creek, to a cold
deep pool filled with slow fat frogs.

We aimed for their heads—
splitting skulls, piercing brains.
We became Lee and Harvey,
the Oswald twins.

I forget what ran out first,
the frogs or our ammo. I left
for home feeling grownup,
like my uncle who hunted
deer and would appear
in our driveway, smiling
while showing off some gunned-
down buck—gutted and roped
to the blood splattered roof
of his rusted station wagon.

That night after I had hunkered
down in bed, I closed my eyes,
only to rerun my last kill. I watched
as it tried to swim off, getting just
about out of range, when I shot
and nailed the back of its head.
In death the frog spun and stared
with large blank eyes, a smirk
on its alien face, as the corpse
began to sink. I followed it down.

最后一笑

艾伦·巴拉克

用我装满霰弹的黛茜·温彻斯特
武装自己，我和我住在附近的一个朋友
走出了家门——
懵懵懂懂的孩童四处徘徊
寻找弄得死的玩意。我们一路来到
九哩溪，来到一个冰冷
幽深的池塘，到处是臃肿肥胖而行动迟缓的青蛙。

我们瞄准它们的头——
碎裂的头骨，迸飞的脑髓。
我们成了李和哈威，
那对奥斯瓦尔德双胞胎。

我忘了先用完了什么，
是青蛙还是子弹。回家时
我觉得自己已经长大成人，
就像我那个猎鹿并出现在
我们归途中的叔叔一样，微笑着
当他炫耀那些被击中的
雄鹿——被开膛破肚后吊在
他那锈迹斑斑的四轮马车
溅满鲜血的顶棚上。

那天晚上，我躺在
床上，我闭上眼睛，
只为了回想我大开杀戒的最后一幕。我看着它
当它试图游走，快要游出
枪的射程时，我开了枪
击中了它的后脑。
这只死了的青蛙快速地旋转着，睁着
大大的、茫然的眼睛，它异样的脸上
泛出一丝傻笑，就在尸体
开始下沉之际。我注视着它下沉。
那笑渐渐变成了一丝牢牢地

The grin grew to a sick smile
that held me fast, until we fell
through the murk and into the cold
black that's found nine miles down.

抓住我的
坏笑，直到我们
在黑暗里落入冰冷
漆黑中才发现已经落下九哩

平安夜
黄芳

我早早来到教堂。
为了一排排的椅子还空。
风琴上长而透明的手，搁着。
黑色封面的《圣经》，
被风吹开又合上。

小小的祷告室里，薄垫安静。
——无数次的低眉和满眶泪水，是我的。
祷告本上反复的字，是我的：
"请给我一碗清水，洗去悲伤与尘埃。
把爱与仇恨引上更洁净的路。"

平安夜，我早早地离开教堂。
因为相信有宁静的祝福，
抵达暗与卑微、疾痛与张望。
——让善的更善。让恶的，
衣衫褴褛。

Christmas Eve
Huang Fang

I arrive at the chapel early.
So there will still be empty seats.
Above, a long crystal hand on the organ.
Black "Bible" on the title page,
blown by wind and closed again.

Tiny prayers in the room, thin cushion calm.
——eyes fill with tears countless times, mine.
Words of the prayer book over and over, mine:
"Please give me a bowl of water, to wash away the dust
                                                    of my sorrow.
Guide love and hate on the road to greater purity."

Christmas Eve, I leave the chapel early.
Because of faith in quiet blessings,
arrive in secret humility, pain, looking around.
——Let kind be kinder. Evil,
clothed in rags.

Our Lady
Patricia Goodrich

I bring her home with me, Our Lady of Guadalupe radiant, ringed with maize yellow, standing on an angel's wings, robe falling in turquoise folds over a clay red gown. Covered from head to toe, only her face shows, lighter than I would expect. How can its two dots and slash create so much feeling? The cherub's face upon whose wings she stands elevates her. We know she is no longer earthly.

Her pure colors and simple lines draw my eyes to her. But when I hold her, it is my hands that take her to my breast. It might be the smoothness of the enamel pink. I like to think it is the carver's hands, shaping and sanding, feeling his way. The clerk at St. Francis de Assisi's gift shop writes out his name, *Leo Jeanette*, local to Ranchos de Taos. A blessing from Our Lady on us both.

我们的圣女
帕特丽夏 · 古德里奇

我把她带回家，我们的瓜达鲁普圣女，周身笼罩着玉米黄光晕，站在一个小天使的翅膀上，罩衣垂下，青绿的褶裥叠在泥红的长袍上。从头到脚包裹着，只露出面容，比想象中更明亮。为何它的两个圆点和一条斜线会创造那么多的情感？那小天使的脸庞使她升腾。我们知道她已不再是凡人。

她纯洁的颜色和简洁的线条吸引着我的眼睛。可是当我抱着她，是我的手把她捧到我的胸前。也许是釉彩里粉红的油滑。我愿意把它看做雕刻匠的手，在塑造着形态，在用砂纸磨擦，感受着他的工作。在阿西斯的圣弗朗斯西礼物店，一个店员写下了他的名字，里奥 · 让奈，塔奥牧场的本地人。这是圣女对我俩的祝福

桃花

杨晓芸

说说盛开的桃花，它的红润过于诱人
我从桃花树下走过，树干粗砺。我不说出
此刻的欢颜与内心的距离
我只说桃花开了，一大片一大片迫不及待地
如同亲爱的我遭遇你
如同三月乳臭，齿痒发作
而非一夜春雨后的溃败，而非欲盖弥彰

peach blossom

Yang Xiaoyun

Speaking of peach blossom blooming, its juicy red too tempting
I pass by under a peach tree, tree trunk rough. I don't speak
the distance between the smile and my inmost being
I only say peach blossom blooms, a large slice of a large slice
                                            moves me
as if I meet you my dear
like the sour smell of March milk, starts teeth itching
but not shattering defeat after one night of Spring rain,
                not the more one hides the more one is exposed

毛妹，店

冉仲景

野娘们，来坛烧酒
两盏温柔
酥花生焖胡豆拌黄瓜炒青椒卤牛肉
不问贵贱尽管上来
今夜我好胃口

我来自古代来自荒村
人饥马乏
成锭的悲哀我一时半会舍不得花
这些散碎的岁月
够吗？

三碗五碗八九碗
痛饮你烈性的微笑，品咂你
59度的问候
我要月亮发毛
要你高高挑起的幌子一生不收

不准吹灯，不准打烊
不准把东倒西歪的山河扶上牙床
野娘们，即使我
紧握哨棒
也不准你放虎归山

马灯开路，暴雨殿后
野娘们，上酒——

Mao Mei, shop
Ran Zhongjing

Wild women, at an earthen jar of brandy
two tender cups
shortbread peanut oil tofu cucumber sauté green pepper
                                        brined beef
expensive or inexpensive
tonight I have a good appetite

I come from ancient Huangcun
hungry man tired horse
saddened for a moment, how can I bear to spend
those scattered
broken years?

three cups five cups eight nine cups
drink your potent smile down, savor your
59 degrees with respect
I want the moon to grow hair
want to excite you not to accept the appearance of a lifetime

You are forbidden to blow out the lamp,
forbidden to burn the midnight oil
forbidden to stagger up the landscape of Fushang and Yuchuan
wild women, even if I press
you are not permitted to let the tiger return to the mountain

Madeng road, rainstorms behind temple
wild women, brandy——

Renovations at the Santuario de Guadalupe
Nathan Brown

Jesus is on his back
on the grand piano while
workers repaint the santuario.

He's an old, time-worn
piece of wood with chips
on the knees, one on the forehead—
white scabs on one tough man-God.

The painters turn off
the mariachi music on a
white-splattered radio, so we
can discuss sacred images.

And I notice, through the scaffolding,
the nails look as if they go through
his feet, the cross, and into the piano,

and his head, normally bowed
when the cross is upright, looks now
as if he's trying to get up.

翻新德瓜达卢佩圣殿

内森·布朗

耶稣躺在
巨大的钢琴上面
而工人们在重新粉刷圣殿。

他是一块历经沧桑的老木头
膝盖上生出木屑，
前额上结着——
这个坚强的人—上帝身上的白痂。

传来墨西哥街头音乐
粉刷工关掉了
溅满白漆的收音机，于是我们
可以讨论圣像。

穿过脚手架，我注意到，
钉子似乎刺穿了
他的脚和十字架，扎进钢琴里，

他的头，在十字架直立时
通常低垂着，现在
他似乎正试着抬起头来。

Onion Creek, Fall
David Meischen

Closing the last gate shut
behind us, we descend
into a hush of cool grey shadow
and cool grey silt. Stepping around
clusters of prickly pear (their spiny fandance),
we take in the slow crumble
of limestone, seashell whisper
of silence against agarita's sharp edges,
intermittent bellowing of cattle
down among the scrub oak,
drowsing the afternoon away
beside a creekbed damp with promise.

洋葱河，秋天
大卫·麦森

关闭我们身后的
最后一扇门，我们步入
一片沉静——凉爽灰白的树荫，
凉爽灰白的淤泥。信步走在
长满小刺的梨树丛中（它们带刺的扇形舞蹈[2]），
我们领会石灰石
慢慢的破碎，海贝壳对着
伏牛花的锋刃默默耳语，
从长满灌木的橡树间
传来断断续续的牛叫声，
打着瞌睡，度过午后的时光，
小河床旁，现着潮湿的生机。

---

[2]　译者注：原文中为"fandance"，词形近似于"fandango"。后者
　　指一种西班牙舞蹈，由一对男女表演，用吉他和响板伴奏。

庭院
李森

庭院，一个词的深渊，比真实的鸟巢大些
我只想把一点苦恼放在我的诗句里
把几株植物，种在我的门槛里
我要在树下，等待从月光里游来的鱼群
我要向鱼群学习语言，学习空虚中的从容
鱼群，把我带走吧，趁着明月的真诚
鱼群，让我长出月光般的鳞片吧
趁着夜色，趁着我还没有破译水井中的波纹

courtyard
Li Sen

courtyard, a word abyss, larger than a real bird nest
I just want to put a little anguish in my poem
grow a few plants on my threshold
I will stand under the tree, wait for a school of fish to swim out from
                                                    the moonlight
I will study the language of the fish, learn to be at ease in the void
fish, take me away, while the bright moon is sincere
fish, let me grow scales like moonbeams
in the dark night, before I decode the ripples in the well

train in the desert at night
Steven Schroeder

after an O'Keeffe at the Amarillo Museum of Art

Nothing catches her eye, one light
yellow in an ocean of it. Steam
eddies trail to the limit of sight,
shatter rainbows on every edge. White
light is nothing of the kind. It is a mass
of rainbows uncontained in blue
and yellow strokes that draw eyes
to it like a cloud troubling sky.

She draws the eye with light, and pigment
plays on paper in the wake of it. Night
washes top to bottom gray to pale
with no horizon. Three lines
draw a teardrop train to a city
off the page. Nothing caught her eye
here. She did not forget.

行驶在沙漠夜色中的列车

史蒂文·施罗德

（在埃默里洛艺术博物馆欣赏奥基弗的作品后）

没有什么能吸引她的目光，
一束黄色的光线在光的海洋里。
气流形成的旋涡望不到尽头，
边缘上处处撒落碎裂的彩虹。
白光和它们完全不同。
一片彩虹在蓝黄交织的涂画中
尽情释放
就像一片困扰天空的云朵
吸引着人们的目光。

她的目光随着光线移动，而颜料
随之嬉戏于纸上。无尽的黑夜
上上下下洗刷着从灰到白
的一切色彩。三根线条
牵引着伤心的列车驶向
陌生的城市。
这里没有什么抓得住
她的目光。
但她不会遗忘。

卡夫卡

刘春

还有什么不能被展览？还有什么
不会被吃掉？我在笼子里撕我的身体
围观者在笼外啃他们的良心
我的胃在冒火，而他们比我更饥饿

这是命，时代的肺结核
感染上面目模糊的祖国。再也没有什么
值得讨论的了，结果早已被商定
广场上，乡村医生对人群举起了针筒

我曾用十年的光阴构造一个国度
它的肮脏与黑暗、它的光明与向往
它许诺过自由，而现在它在咳嗽——
开往纽约的列车停下了引擎

如果留下，我可以做一个称职的保险公司办事员
（但做不了合格的儿子与兄长）；如果
要成为一个"人"，那么只有先变成甲虫
在被遗弃之前，自己流放自己

而我需要的不是食物，不是药剂，是一场审判
秋风中舞动的心，需要一个解释
人变成甲虫算得了什么？
甲虫变成人，这世界才会睁大它的眼球！

"烧掉这些不合时宜的纸张吧，
更不要为它们添上结尾。"这是
倦怠者对现实的否决，是普通公民的尝试——
他是否有资格支配自己的一生？

Kafka
Liu Chun

What can't be put on public display? What
can't be consumed? Caged, I tear my body
onlookers outside the cage gnaw on their consciences
my belly's on fire, but they are more hungry than I

This is life, a time of tuberculosis
infecting the indistinct face of the motherland. There is nothing
worth discussing, since it was decided long ago
in the public square, country doctors raised syringes to treat a crowd

some time ago I used up ten years of valuable time in a country
that is dark and dirty, longing for light
it promises freedom, but now it coughs——
New York bound train stops its engine

if I remain, I may be a competent insurance clerk
(though unable to cope with endless eligible sons and brothers); does
one become a "person," only when one earlier became a beetle
before being abandoned, one's own exile one's own

but I don't need food, medicine, I need a place to be put on trial
heart dancing in autumn wind, need an explanation
must people become beetles?
When beetles become people this world will open its eyes wide!

"Burn these unsuitable papers,
do not add a coda to the end." One
who rejects reality is worn out, ordinary citizens try——
does anyone have authority to dominate a whole life?

Downtown Albuquerque
Aaron Rudolph

Pat and I traveled to the city
with all the concrete and buildings.
We'd come from our little town early
so Pat, who sped his way through the city's
streets a few months before, could square
himself with the court system. A block
from the courthouse, a gray-haired man,
arms and legs as slack as branches,
performed Tai Chi in the morning air.
Around us, cars whizzed by, sputtered
smoke and honked horns, sounds
of a thousand wounded dogs.

"Some crazy nut," Pat said about the guy
and we walked away. But I was thinking
of the man as a piñon tree rooted
in the forest; the wind pushing
through it. The tree looks natural
there, an object in the background that heightens
the scene: a careful brushstroke.

爱伯克奇市中心

阿龙·鲁道夫

帕特和我进城
那里充满混凝土和建筑物。
早早地，我们从小镇赶来
帕特，几个月前曾驱车超速
穿越这座城市的街道，
此时，可以向法院体系低头。
在离法院一个街区的地方，
一个头发灰白的男人，
胳膊和腿，像树枝一样松弛，
在清晨的空气中，打着太极。
在我们四周，汽车呼啸而过，呼呼
冒烟，
喇叭响个不停，听起来
像是上千只受伤的狗在哀嚎。

"一个疯子，"帕特说那个家伙
之后我们走开。但我在想
那个人是一棵松树扎根在森林里；
风穿过它。那棵树站在那里
看起来，自然而然。
城市背景里的一个客体
更加突显那画面：匠心独具的一笔。

机关枪新娘

唐丹鸿

那是纯洁的燃烧的星期几?
穿高统丝袜的交叉的美腿一挺
我吹哨:机关枪新娘,机关枪
你转动了我全身的方向盘
你命令我驶向了疯人院

那是东边的火药瞄准西边的头发
那是愤怒的朝霞插入扳机的食指
那是大丽花突然抬起微风捂住乳房
那是你,把钢琴剧痛的脂肪往下按

你的裸体在锉子六月下泛蓝
你的叹息给铜管乐划了一把叉
但愿我的鼻子形同手掌
机关枪新娘,机关枪
远远地,我抱着你的肩,捧着上面的香水

我是反光纠缠着钥匙私语
我是正光抽打的无知的阉人
我是闪身让你加速的高速公路
我是棉花、水银和……呜咽

machine gun bride
Tang Danhong

which pure, flaming day is this?
silk stockings straightened long lovely legs crossed
I blow the whistle: machine gun bride, machine gun
you turn the wheel of my whole body
you order me to sail toward the madhouse

it is east gun powder aiming at west hair
it is fiery red clouds putting a finger on the trigger
it is a dahlia rising on sudden breeze to cover breasts
it is you, pounding the fat of the throbbing piano head down

your naked body burns blue under a June file
your sigh marks off brass
if only my nose were like the palm of the hand
machine gun bride, machine gun
I hold your shoulders, cup perfume over them

I am reflected light tangled around a whispering key
I am direct light whipping ignorant castrati
I am the highway that dodges so you can go faster
I am cotton, quicksilver...sob

Pastoral
Alysa Hayes

Perhaps, I fit,
am a pond swept clean by the wind
and the murmur of winter wheat
rubbing along the weeds.
This far out, there is no crowd to unsettle me—
no road, no rustic shack
or paradise on the horizon—
just the lines converging
to one point at my feet.

Far off, the factory lies
slumped and abandoned, unnoticed by most.
I've seen the tracks there where some
have climbed the rough steel by moonlight
to smother their kisses in necks and palms.
They could not escape the fairytales either,
and went up eagerly,
as if they'd defeated some great ogre
to make love on his corpse.

I stand here sunlit, whistling
as I do on the 24
while my face crackles in the glass
against a blur of lights.
The window rides a mirage
through each stranger's shoulders,
and we jumble, afraid of breaking
our silence like a fisted can.
Some mumble indifferently to the night.
I send my tune into the wind.
Somehow, I thought it would be different.
The morning mist burnt before I arrived.
The man-monster shines clear, cold,
and distant.

田园

艾莉莎·海斯

或许，我正是
被风拂净的池塘
和冬麦的私语
摩挲着野草。
这辽远之地，没有人群使我忐忑不安——
没有道路，没有粗糙的棚户
或是将要出现的天堂——
只有脚下的线条
汇成一点。

工厂横在远方，
衰败而荒废，被人们漠视。
我看见不远处的铁轨，在那里
人们乘着月光爬上粗砺的钢铁
掩盖脖颈和手掌上的吻。
他们同样无法逃离童话，
他们激情澎湃。
就像他们打败了可怕的妖魔
并在他的尸体上做爱。

我站在这里，晒着太阳，吹着口哨。
正如我二十四岁那年
我的脸在玻璃的微弱光线里
噼啪作响。
在每个陌生人的肩头
窗户驾驭着一个海市蜃楼，
我们混杂，唯恐像个握拳的罐头一样
打破沉默。
人们漠然地对着黑夜喃喃低语。
我把我的曲调送入风中。
不知为何，我想它也许会不同。
晨雾在我到来之前燃烧。
人形魔鬼清晰地闪耀，冰冷，
而又遥远。

爱情和马
吉木狼格

草原上只有马
它们吃草，交配和奔跑
阳光灿烂
这快乐的表达
激起了我的不满
而阳光确实灿烂
我躺在草原上
制造虚构的悲哀
让目光把自己送到天上
马不会，马在草原深处
交配和奔跑
我躺着（在天上）
必然孤单
除非灵魂随一阵风
朝马群扑去

我在只有马的地方
幻想爱情
当一匹母马朝我走来
说不定我会羞怯

love and horse
Jimu Langge

on the prairie only horses
they graze, copulate, and gallop
the sun is bright
this cheery expression
excites my resentment
yet the sun really is bright
I lie on the prairie
making up grief
let me fly on the wings of eyes
the horse won't, the horse deep down on the prairie
will copulate and gallop
I lie (in the sky)
inevitably lonely
unless with a gust of wind my soul
dashes into the horses

in the place with horses only I
fantasize love
if a mare approaches me
maybe I will blush

That Which Clings
Kenneth Hada

Stick-tights cling to socks
leggings and boot strings
as I explore emptiness,
this absent space
this presence,
these jutting rocks
on the sauntering plain,
the dying briars
matted against red rock
and prickly pair,
bluestem dancing
in haunted rhythms
under a diminished sun,
lingering daylight.

I walk this vapid prairie
sensing vacancies within,
discerning essence,
the self whole, defined
in September wind
scolding, consoling:
there are things learned
only by failure
and things failed
despite the learning.

那紧缠的
肯尼斯·哈达

鬼针草紧缠短袜
裤袜和靴带
我探索虚空，
这不在场的空间
这在场，
这些突出的岩石
在悠然漫步的平原上，
垂死的石南
缠绕赤岩
易怒的一对，
舞动的须芒草
中了邪的节奏
羸弱的太阳下，
日光迟迟不落。

走在这了无生趣的草原上
感知其中的虚空，
识辨本质，
完整的自我，轮廓显现
在九月的风中
谩骂着，抚慰着：
有些事情
只能从失败中学习
事情失败了
尽管在学习。

夸耀
冉仲景

不论肥沃还是硗碡，这土地
都是种子的。而种子，是上天的
秋天，我有颗粒无收的诗篇

不知道哪位淘气的神仙
把星光全吹灭了
今夜，我有黑灯瞎火的爱情

从果演算到花，我有错
寒潮来袭，我有冷
山那边仍然是山啊，我有远

原野茫茫，四面八方都在召唤
升天也好，落草也罢
走与投，我有路

谁能说我不曾修造房屋
幕天席地，我的建筑多么壮观
我有门，我有窗

帷幕刚启，鸟兽虫鱼
便簇拥着死亡之神来到舞台中央
此生，我有来不及的微笑

exaltation
Ran Zhongjing

fertile or sterile, this soil
is seeded. And seeds are heaven's
Autumn, I have poetry with no harvest

don't know which mischievous immortal
blew out starlight
tonight, I have love that is blind

counting from fruits to flowers, I was wrong
a cold spell comes in, I am cold
ah, beyond hills still hills, I am distant

wild boundless plain, ancestors call from all directions
to ascend to heaven, or withdraw to woods
to go or be reborn, I have ways

who says I didn't build a house
sky is my roof and earth is my mat, how splendid it is
I have doors, I have windows

curtains just opened, bird beast insect fish
escort the god of death to center stage
in this life, I have no time to smile

West of Fort Worth
Scott Wiggerman

The rim of the horizon
blisters in purple hues,
exposes an expanse
of land as flat as an iron,
not entirely empty—fences,
hubcaps, billboards for Jesus,
a rare gas station or taqueria—
an odd look of abandonment,
perhaps the way the land was
before stagecoaches and settlers,
trading posts and saloons;
perhaps before conquistadors
or even the Comanche,
a hearty rolling prairie
of cinnamon and harvest green,
of hidden hollows, old,
not vintage, when land
was more precious than man.

沃斯城堡以西

司各特·威格曼

地平线的边缘
起了紫色的疤,
袒露广袤大地
平如钢铁,
不全是空的——栅栏,
汽车的毂盖,耶稣招贴画,
一个罕见的加油站或者玉米饼店——
一片古怪的荒凉景象,
可能这片土地在
公共马车和定居者,
贸易点和沙龙之前;
可能在占领者
甚至是科曼切人之前,
是肥沃丰饶而绵延起伏的草原,
有肉桂树和丰收的绿色,
隐蔽的洼地,古老
但不是古董,那时
土地比人类珍贵。

Blue Norther
Larry Thomas

At high noon,
brutal as a boot
kicked into the groin
of indolence,

it hits,
tattooing the cheeks
of cowhands
with frostbite,

locking the eyes
of hawks
wide-open
with a glaze

of clear blue ice
freezing their bodies
upright to the tops
of fence posts,

terrorizing
the bleak
West Texas
desertscape

like a huge
blue falcon
loosed from the wrist
of God.

蓝色北风

赖里·托马斯

正午，
残忍如靴子
踢进了
倦怠的阴部，

令人疼痛，
在牧牛人的脸上
留下刺青般的痕迹
和冻疮，

锁定鹰的
眼睛
圆睁着
呆板的

透明的蓝冰层
冻得他们的身体
直挺挺地立在
篱柱的顶端

使荒凉的
德克萨斯西部的
沙漠景观
满目狰狞

就像一只巨大的
蓝色猎鹰
从神的腕部
放飞。

重阳登高
瞿永明
——遍插茱萸少一人

思亲问题 友爱问题
一切问题中最动人的
全都是登高的问题
都是会当临绝顶时
把盏的问题

今朝一人 我与谁长谈?
遥望远处 据称是江北
白练入川是一条，还是两条?
汇向何处 都让我喜欢

在江北以远 是无数美人
男人们登高 都想得到她们
尽管千年之内 哺乳动物
和人类 倒一直
保持着生态平衡

今朝我一人把盏 江山变色
青色三春消耗了我
九九这个数字 如今又要
轮回我的血脉
远处一俯一仰的山峰
赤裸着跳入我怀中
我将只有毫无用处地
享受艳阳

mountain climbing on double nine day
Zhai Yongming

each a dogwood and my branch missing (Wang Wei)

homesickness question   friendship question
of all questions the most touching
is the mountain climbing question
all about the summit reaching
raising wine cups question

now alone   I offer whom a long talk?
you can see in the distance   it is said north of the Yangtze
does the silver river enter Sichuan one, or still two?
wherever it flows   I like it anyway

deep into the north of the river   live countless beauties
whenever men climb mountains   they miss them
although for a thousand years   mammals
and humans   always
live in harmony

now when I raise the cup alone   landscape changes color
three green months of spring consume me
this double nine   nowadays wants again
to flow in my veins
the peaks far away, one bowing, one looking up
leap into my arms naked
I shall lack all capacity
to enjoy bright sunshine

思伤脾 醉也伤脾
飒飒风声几万？ 呼应谁来临？
饮酒入喉 它落到身体最深处
情欲和生死问题
离别和健康问题
也入喉即化 也落到最深处
它们变得敏捷 又绵密
它们醉了 也无处不在

一九九九．九月初九登南京栖霞山

190

thinking harms the spleen   drinking also harms the spleen
how many thousand rustling winds?   upon whose arrival?
wine slips down the throat   into the deepest part of the body
desire mixes with life and death question
separation mixes with health question
melt as soon as they sink down the throat   into the deepest part
they become nimble   soft and dense
they get drunk   also nowhere not in

摆手舞曲：春天
舟仲景

领口太小，月季脱衣
雨水太涩，燕子写信
土豆花开了一朵一朵又一朵
第四朵说请等一等
眉苏河边，太阳停下梳头
酒酣时分，百合学习接吻
铁匠家的四个闺女
一起把对面山坡拉到膝头
她们要用怎样的针线
才能绣出昨日梦境——
杏依偎着桃，篱牵挂着藤
天底下，到处都是相爱的人

hand-waving dance: spring
Ran Zhongjing

collar too tight, Chinese rose takes off her clothes
rain too bitter, swallow writes a letter
potato blossoms one one again one
fourth says please wait
alongside the river, sun stops to comb hair
drunk on wine, lily learns to kiss
blacksmith's four virgin daughters
gather hillside opposite
what needles and lines would they use to
embroider yesterday's dream——
almonds snuggle up to peaches, and fence leads vine
under heaven, everyone everywhere is in love

prevailing time
Steven Schroeder

Red earth waits in new furrows for wind
to carry it away to Monahans.

It migrates like birds on instinct, on prevailing
time. I just flew in from Winter, and Spring

plows seem out of place. But sun swears snow
is gone, and light almost never lies

at this altitude. Blades in threes get drunk
on wind. Grassfires make ashes
for a penitential season.

盛行的时令
史蒂文 · 施罗德

红土在新开的犁沟中等待
风会将它带到莫纳汉斯。

它就像候鸟在盛行的时令本能地迁徙。
我仅是从冬天飞进这盛行的时令里，

春犁似乎不合时宜。但太阳发誓
冰雪已逝，而光线几乎从不撒谎

在这样的高度。风中的叶片
醉意渐浓。为了这个忏悔的季节
燎原之火生成灰烬。

债务
冉仲景

有时是雨水，有时是铁钉
春天刚刚开始
我就欠了阳雀一刻倾听

种子发芽，田野肌肉拉伤
我还欠老牛一把嫩草
欠蝴蝶一绺阳光

站在高高的苍岭上
我还欠兀鹰一句回答
欠远方一次眺望

灯前，我垂下头来
前世今生
我一直欠着自己一条河流

debt
Ran Zhongjing

sometimes rain, sometimes nails
just now, spring began
I owe cuckoo a listen

seeds sprout, field's muscles strain
I owe old cow a handful of tender grass
owe butterfly a strand of sunshine

high on the green mountain
I owe eagle an answer
owe distance a gaze

under the lamp, head down
from my last life to this one
I have always owed myself a river

瓦蓝瓦蓝的天空
李南

那天河北平原的城市，出现了
瓦蓝瓦蓝的天空。
那天我和亲爱的，谈起了青海故乡

德令哈的天空和锦绣，一直一直
都是这样。
有时我想起她，有时又将她遗忘

想起她时我的心儿就微微疼痛
那天空的瓦蓝，就像思念的伤疤
让我茫然中时时惊慌

忘记她时我就楚身走进黯淡的生活
忙碌地爱着一切，一任巴音河的流水
在远处日夜喧响。

pastel blue sky
Li Nan

On that day over Hebei plain's city, appeared
a pastel blue sky.
On that day, a dear friend and I talked about our home, Qinghai

Delingha's sky and silk clouds, always always
are like this.
Sometimes I recall her, sometimes I forget.

When I recall her I feel pangs in my heart
Sky's pastel blue, like the scar of absence
leaves me lost and confused

When I forget her, I turn and enter gray life
busily love everything, let the Bayin River's water
drone day and night in a distant place.

红土高原

李森

站着，我的脚下
就是红土高原
眼前的那排桉树
粗大的和丑陋的
早已在我的心中
繁殖着枝条
结下了一箩筐球果
只是我不曾觉察

穿花夹克衫的知了
也在我的心中长大
直到它们挂在树叶上
直到它们叫醒了我

是的，我的眼前
就是红土高原
桉树围着一座农舍
知了还在不停地叫着夏天
而我却开始回忆
春天的一棵树根
在潮湿的红土里
绕开磐石

是啊，我就是变成一只鸟
永远在天上飞
变成一头豹子
不停地在山中跑
也看不见
整个美丽的高原

但是，所有穿花夹克衫的知了
都已经长大
它们叫醒了我之后
就挂在桉树叶上沉默

red earth plateau
Li Sen

standing, beneath my feet
is the red earth plateau
that row of eucalyptus trees before my eyes
thick ones, ugly ones
long ago in my heart
branches grew
yielded a basket of fruit
only without my noticing it

cicadas in flowery jackets
have also grown up in my heart
up until they cling to leaves in trees
up until they wake me

yes, before my own eyes
in the red earth plateau
a farmhouse is surrounded by eucalyptus trees
cicadas chatter endlessly in summer
and I step back to recollect
a tree root in Spring
in damp red earth
going around huge rocks

yes, even if I become a bird
flying forever in the sky
become a leopard
always running in the mountains
still I will not see
the whole beautiful plateau

nevertheless, the cicadas in flowery jackets
have all grown up
have clung since they woke me
to the leaves of eucalyptus trees in silence

Low Pressure
Patricia Goodrich

First, clouds- not nebuli or strata- the large cotton cumulus, tinged with gray, signal the change, and what should have been rain comes as wind, whipping the bleak day like an old woman beating her rugs.

I come back heavier than I left-silt crusted scalp, eyes red rimmed, dust-powdered skin sanded like a pine board. Yet, leaning into the wind, my body sends a message: *This is familiar. This is the New Mexico I knew.*

More than architecture, more than sky, my first days blessed by a blue that people here paint their gates to keep evil away, this wind's wail and buffet speaks to me.

低压
帕特丽夏·古德里奇

起初，云朵——不是星云或云层——棉花般的大朵积云，略带灰色，发出变化的信号，本该有雨，风却来了，鞭打这阴郁的一天，像个老妇在抽打她的小地毯。

我归来，比离去时更沉重——淤泥结成壳的头皮，眼睛镶着红色，灰扑扑的皮肤像块撒满沙子的松木板。可是，在风中倾斜，我的身躯传递一条信息：这很熟悉。这是我熟知的新墨西哥。

不只是建筑，不只是天空，我最初的日子为蓝色所保佑，这里的人们把门漆成蓝色来驱邪避灾，这风的尖叫和吹袭在对我诉说。

当天晚上
海男

当天晚上，不冒危险的选择了一个有利的预兆
国家在夜晚的单纯为我们提供了一种工具
现在，我绝不会想起沙漠上的女人
绝不会想起老练的马匹、博取过我们的友谊
这个夜晚，甘蔗酒和野心
一直照射着，谦虚的口吻，悄悄地想爬上去
没有一条溪流可以挂上一面镜子
可以取出伤疤，倦容和新的疵子的干扰
有人冒过险吗？为海洋、一匹奔驰的马、一块
街心花园
有人冒过险么？为魔鬼、为炼金士，一种广泛
的哲学
而那正在冒险的人为什么是诗人
而不是一条河、一个渴得难熬的孕妇

that night
Hai Nan

That night, taking no risk we chose a good omen
the State's innocence at night gives us a sort of tool
right now, I certainly can't remember the desert woman
can't remember the old horse that befriended us
this night, sugarcane liquor and wild ambition
burning continually, modest speech quietly climbs
no small stream serves as a mirror
to remove scars, fatigue, the nuisance of new blemishes
Has anyone gone in search of adventure? The sea a galloping horse
a garden in the middle of the street
Has anyone gone in search of adventure? A demon an alchemist
a wide-ranging philosophy
and why is the adventurer on the road a poet
not a river not an unbearably thirsty pregnant woman

色达草原

何小竹

我没去过色达草原
我只是听说过色达草原
因为色达这名字好听
我就记住了
我记住色达草原已经多年
现在我已把色达草原
当做一个回忆
我回忆色达草原的时候
主要是用舌尖反复模拟
色达这两个音节
除此之外
别的景物都想象不起来
我深深地为色达草原着迷
却依然想象不出
那应该是什么样的草原

Seda Prairie
He Xiaozhu

I haven't been to Seda Prairie
I have only heard of Seda Prairie
because the name Seda sounds nice
I remember it
I've remembered Seda Prairie for many years
now I've regarded Seda Prairie
as a memory
when I recall Seda Prairie
I mainly use the tip of my tongue to keep mimicing
the two syllables Se da
apart from this
I recollect nothing
I'm deeply intoxicated with Seda Prairie
but still cannot imagine
what kind of prairie it should be

Woody Guthrie Memorial Highway
Steven Schroeder

sign just beyond the intersection
of Faulkner and the railroad
track has me singing
so long, thinking dust bowl.

It's dry. A cache of fuel
the size of Rhode Island and wind
enough to drive it to the end
of vision. No wonder the cows
don't move. They've seen nothing
like it their whole lives and know
there's nowhere to go.

Just stand
in wind,
whole offering.

树木茂密的高斯里公路

史蒂文·施罗德

刚过福克纳十字路口的路标
而铁道
使我放声歌唱，
久久地，回想起积尘盆地。

那里很干旱。不过一箱燃料
加上吹过的风
足以让我们驰骋在这罗德岛大小的地方
驶向视野穷尽的地方。难怪尘风中的牛群
一动不动。它们一生从未见识过
类似的怪物并知道
无路可走。

只是站在
风中，
完全献祭。

almost human
Steven Schroeder

grassfire
brushes off grass,
rushes headlong nowhere

in particular,
consumes all
it can while
every other
thing there
wonders

at its hunger
at its hunger

近乎人类
史蒂文·施罗德

草燃烧
除掉草，
闷头向前冲，无处

可以藏身，
吞噬所有
能吞下的
而那里
每一件
其它事物
都惊愕于

它的饥饿
它的饥饿

西昌的月亮
吉木狼格

如果我说西昌的月亮
像一个荡妇
正人君子会骂我流氓
如果我说西昌的月亮
像一个流氓
人们会笑我胡说
皓月当空的时候
我站在（坐着也行）
月光下看一本书
连标点符号都清晰可见
西昌的月亮什么也不像
它只是很大

Xichang moon
Jimu Langge

if I say the Xichang moon
is like a whore
gentlemen will call me a hooligan
if I say the Xichang moon
is like a hooligan
folks will laugh my nonsense away
when the bright moon hangs in the sky
I stand (sitting will also do)
and read a book in the moonlight
even punctuation marks are clearly visible
Xichang moon is like nothing
it's just really big

Full Moon, Cirrocumulus, Light Breeze, and Iridescence
Wendy Barker

Ocean and crater,
iris, wide pupil,
until a thread, a clump
of cloud startling
the way a car door
thumps closed, the face
turned to the wheel,
down the drive,
gone. And silence
as a canoe slides
past the dock at dusk,
the plash of the paddle,
ripple of water, tip
of the prow drifting
beyond a branch,
the planks under us
even now rocking.

满月、卷积云、清风和虹彩

温迪·巴克

海洋和火山口，
虹膜、宽阔的瞳孔，
直到一丝、一团
云彩吓人一跳，
就像车门砰地一声关上
踩上油门，
消失在天边。
而寂静
如独木舟在黄昏时分
划过船坞，
水面泛起涟漪，
船继续漂移，
我们脚下的支板
现在还在摇晃。

虚构的玫瑰
海男

镜子中的月亮，感到一种的虚幻的增加
在南部小镇上一个多年以前曾经忘不掉的人
树叶披散，凡是白天和黑夜的时间
引起秘密的尊敬。我要看见那个秘密的焦急的面孔
宪法和婚姻制度，卧室中一座镀金的房屋
母体和遗婴的出现反映了一本书上的每个词
反映了一个胸口上的石榴、一朵玫瑰
吸引人的潮汐、吸引人的战争、吸引人的身材
诗歌，不可思议地凄凉
最后一个世纪无法回报的虚无
就这样在凹下去的一块承放云团的地方
蚂蚁们驱赶着死的念头

illusive roses
Hai Nan

Moon in the mirror, a sense of illusion rising
in a small southern town lives an unforgettable person
leaves droop, all day all night
secret esteem awakens. I long to see the secret anxious face
marriage institution and contract, gold chamber in the bedroom
mother's body and the motherless child reflect words from a book
reflect a pomegranate in the pit of the stomach, a rose
tempting tide, tempting war, tempting figure
poetry, incredibly desolate
illusion, unrequited by the last century
so in the concave place where clouds are held
ants drive away the idea of dying

干燥的南部山冈

海男

干燥的南部山冈上的气候
只剩下一点一滴的水，春天太早地使人们
前额衰老。我蹲在一个土洼里
低低的土洼，我设想死去后
情人会不会检查出我头发上的细菌
在云南，我从未这样低沉和动摇
但是，镜子照着热气上升的火焰
我变形，扭曲或开始对自己撒谎
又一个妇女走出来埋她的婴儿
我开始将一枚即将收割的麦穗
放在这个未曾长大的女婴身边
她长不大，我却在干燥的气候走下山冈

dry, dry southern hills
Hai Nan

Dry dry climate of low southern hills
leaves drops of water alone, Spring leaves brows wrinkled
before people are old. I crouch on low land
low low land, wonder if after I die
my lover will find the bacteria teeming in my hair
In Yunnan, I have never sunk so low,
but the mirror reflects rising flames
I twist, turn, lie to myself
another woman goes out to bury her baby
I place a head of wheat almost ripe
by the body of the baby girl who will never grow up
she cannot grow up, and I walk in the dry climate down the low hill

Near-Earth Object
Wendy Barker

They said a second moon,
a bright new sphere
orbiting our planet, another
presence we can count on.
Have you seen the moons tonight,
we'll say, they both are full!
And suddenly our small
circumference has swollen
to the size of Saturn's—first
one moon, then two, in time
we might have rings, a crown
of moons all following
the wisps of our transparencies,
the clouds, the drifts of all our storms.
But no—they're saying now
it's the last stage
of an Apollo rocket launched
thirty years ago, returned from
decades revolving round the sun.
A boomerang's ellipsis:
a word we uttered once,
flung back to us.

临近地球的物体

温迪·巴克

他们说，第二个月亮，
一个明亮而崭新的球体
正环绕着我们的星球，又一个存在
我们可以依赖。
今晚，你看见月亮了吗，
我们会说，它们两个都是满月！
突然之间我们渺小的
圆周，膨胀到
土星大小——先是
一个月亮，然后两个，迟早
我们或许会拥有光环，一个
月亮之冠，月亮
全都跟随着我们透明的光速，
还有云层，我们所有风暴的堆积物。
但不——他们现在说
它是，即将寿终正寝的
阿波罗火箭
三十年前发射，环绕太阳
数十年之后归来。
一个回飞镖的省略：
一个我们曾经说出的单词，
最终飞回到我们身边。

Harvest Moon
Larry Thomas

for Deena

It hung in the late
October sky
so big and bright
people everywhere,
just to look at it,
pulled their cars
over to the shoulders
of the roads.

My daughter of two,
clung to my chest
like a monkey,
caught suddenly up
in the throes
of her small body
acting with a mind
of its own, pointed her right

index finger toward the sky,
parted her pursed lips,
and crooned, for the very
first time, sliding off her tongue
like a warm, sweet disk
of butterscotch candy,
the word 'moon,' startling
her so she started crying.

满月
——献给蒂娜

赖里·托马斯

它悬挂在
十月底的夜空
那么大那么亮
四方的人，
只是为了看看它，
把车
停靠在
路肩上。

我两岁的女儿，
依在我怀里
像只小猴，
幼小的身躯
倏然乱动起来
行事全凭主见
她右手食指
指着天空，

张开嗫着的小嘴，
轻轻嘟囔，第一次，
"月亮"这个词，
像一颗温润香甜的
黄油奶糖
从舌头上滑落，
这个词，吓着了她
她开始哭泣。

减法
冉仲景

去年，阳雀叫了五声
今年三声。明年呢？后年呢？

筛眼密密麻麻，谷种何其少
日子剩下许多空壳

稻草：绳子越搓越长
锯子：木材和白昼越来越短

唠叨了一辈子，争论了一辈子
不留下半句遗言

subtraction
Ran Zhongjing

last year, cuckoo cried five times
three this year. next year? the year after?

fine sieve, but grains are scarce
many days chaff remains

straw: long rope twisted
saw: wood and daylight grow short

badgering for a lifetime, a lifetime of bickering
not even a broken word left behind

到底是谁出卖了我
海男

从味道、翩翩舞动的角隅间
散发出我的声音，它们不可能是词语
它们只不过从水的沸腾中，从豆荚的
形态中，宣判了我的性别

用尽可能的纤细，寻找到了器物
它们是容纳了茧和丝的暗房
它们是占据了整个旅途位置的颠覆
它们是承述不清的蝴蝶和它的飞翔

到底是谁出卖了我
在接近暮色时分，我的心脏
像苹果一样饱满，像春色一样迷乱
像出卖我的人一样诡异

who sold me out in the end?
Hai Nan

from the dancing, fluttering corners of flavor
my voice comes, they can't be words
they only come from water boiling, from the shapes of
bean pods, pronounce the sentence of my sex

looking by every possible nuance for tools
they are hidden chambers that contain cocoons and silk
they are the disruption that occupies the whole journey
they are the inexpressible butterfly and its flight

who sold me out in the end?
a moment before twilight, my heart
plump as an apple, colorful as Spring confusion
strange as the one who sold me out

仿佛这忧伤，是真的
黄芳

仿佛这是真的。
那些孤独，
一点点，一点点地沉了下去。

当她提着竹篮盛装的大雾，
从外面回来，那些悲欢
一点点，一点点地浮了起来。

仿佛这是恰如其分的——
阳光中，树枝长高。
黄昏里，桃花凋落。

当青春、爱情、写满隐私的旧纸张，
在深处打转、沉浮。
她转身，不发一言。

——仿佛这忧伤，是真的。

as if this sadness, were real
Huang Fang

As if this were real.
Those lonely,
little by little, sink down.

When she lifts the bamboo basket filled with great fog,
coming back from outside, those sad joyful
little by little, float up.

As if this were no more and no less——
in sunshine, trees grow.
At dusk, peach blossoms fall.

When youth, love, and old personal papers
spin in the depths, sink,
she turns, without a word.

——as if this sadness, were real.

Kite Flying
Sherry Craven

I made love once
and it turned sour,
soulless,
even silly.

New love was
like a puppy
all feet and fuzz,
clumsy and eager,
the child before
adolescence,
the air before
summer rain.

I tried to hold onto passion,
but like a kite
at the end of a string,
desire slipped through
my fingers until
at last I gave up,
and watched you drift
farther and farther away
until I couldn't imagine
new love any more

断线的风筝

雪莉·克莱文

我曾做过一次爱
而它变酸了，
冷漠无情，
甚至愚蠢。

新生的爱情
像一只幼犬
四足站立 满身绒毛，
笨拙而急切，
乳臭未干的
孩子，
夏日暴雨前的
空气。

我试图挽留激情，
但它像线端的
风筝，
渴望从我指缝间
滑脱
直到我最终放弃，
看着你飘得
越来越远
直到我无法再想象
新生的爱情

Cleaving a Valentine
Jerry Bradley

This is no day for distance. Your reward
for six years of sick separation
is these chocolates I send and a card

recalling how much the far-off heart can bear.
Tell me, what is love but what we've conferred
upon ourselves to make our drab lives dear?

And why must these scarlet letters suggest disease?
Still we telephone our passion when we know
valentines are better carved upon trees

(though in West Texas only those planted,
staked, watered by hand, and plotted will grow).
You think I have taken love for granted,

though I contend I have loved you enough
for anyone's life but mine. There's in me,
I say, a pit, a seed of something rough,

too wide and vast to hear its own sad bark.
It grows slow like love but is more enduring
and sturdier than any time-cleft heart.

情人节的断肠人

杰里 · 布拉得雷

这一天应该没有距离。我寄给你
这些巧克力和一张卡片
以补偿你
六年离别之苦

回想着远方之心能够忍受几多痛苦。
我的爱，告诉我，爱情除了调剂我们单调的生活
还能是什么？

这些红色的字母为何定然暗示疾病呢？
我们知道情人节礼物最好刻在树上
却仍然打电话诉说衷肠

（然而在西德克萨斯只有人工栽种，
打桩、浇水、成片的树才会生长）。
你觉得，我想当然地接受了爱情，

尽管我声辩道，除却我自己的生命
我爱你胜过爱一切。
我的体内，
我说，有一个坑，有一粒粗家伙的种子，

宽阔得听不见它自己的哀嚎。
它像爱情一样慢慢生长，但比任何久别的心
都要持久，都要强壮。

Winter Wedding
Alan Berecka

The Texas winter brings brown,
dead trees, bored leaves sterile
rain and mud. It grows and tails
anything dead that moves,
and when it can it swallows.

It followed the guests in their grays
and reds. It followed the groom in his panic.
It followed the priest, quietly. Mud can
be reverent. It followed the bride. It inched
up and stained her white gown. It climbed
her father and ruined his shine. It carried
its reminder: "Dust thou art, until you add water."

During the service, women cried, especially
the mothers. No one noticed the mud or tried
not to, but when they got home or to their rented
rooms, the mud climbed up onto their hands,
and hid beneath their fingernails.

That night the lost cause was joined.
The mud slipped up to and smudged
the unmade sheets. The marriage was final.

The mud still oozes onto the walks, sits
on the steps and stairs, hides in closets
and on us all, waiting for the next feast,
its next chance to swallow.

冬日婚礼
艾伦 · 巴拉克

德克萨斯的冬天带来了棕色，
枯树，布满虫眼的树叶，荒瘠的
雨水和泥土。它蔓延着，跟随着
任何僵死的、移动的物体
它伺机吞噬。

它跟随，穿灰衣或红衣的宾客。
它跟随，惊慌失措的新郎。
它跟随着神父，悄悄地。泥土也能
毕恭毕敬。它跟随着新娘。它一点点
往上弄脏了洁白的婚纱。它爬上
她父亲的身体，玷污了他的光辉。它裹挟着
它的提示："你本是尘土，直到你加入水。"

仪式中，女人们哭泣，尤其是
母亲们。没有人注意到泥土或者试图
忽视它，可当他们回到家里或租来的
房间里，泥爬上了他们的手，
藏匿在他们的指甲盖下。

那个晚上，是失意的结合。
泥土偷偷地爬上凌乱的床单
弄脏它。婚礼结束了。

泥土仍然流溢在走道上，端坐在
台阶和楼梯上，藏在壁橱里
以及我们所有人的身上，等待着下一次盛宴，
下一个吞噬的机会。

Yu's Wife
Natasha Marin

When the great flood came to China, he left to claw riverbeds between fields of young rice. The old men say he has made one thousand streams like slivers in the soil. The water can not feel its own wet heart – it bleeds too thin. They smell the air and sketch at the dust with sharp bamboo. Their pity stinks like charred fish skin. Their moon eyes lie to me but thin lips mumble that I should feel proud that the current slinks slower than a salamander, next to his quick wrists.

Wise Night:
has he forgotten me?
    Nine years gone
like the curve of a woman's calf
    into the warm salt sea.
Brave Stars,
    look to the skylark
    before blinking down at me.
See how the West Wind
calls wings to fickle trysts –
    and so convinced that only his cold breath will hold her –
    the skylark will choose love
        over stillness.

禹的妻子

娜塔莎·马林

巨大的洪流向中国涌来，他选择了留下，用双手在禾苗青青的田地之间开凿河床。老人说：他已经凿出了一千条小河，棉条般蜿蜒于大地上。河水感受不到它自己湿润的心脏——它细若游丝。它们闻嗅着空气，用尖尖的竹子素描尘埃。它们的怜悯就像被烤焦的鱼皮散发出异味。它们月亮般的眼睛对我撒谎，但是薄薄的嘴唇却在咕哝：他雷厉风行，水流溜得比螺蟮慢，我应该引以为豪。

睿智的黑夜：
他已忘了我吗？
         九年光景过去了
就像女人小腿肚的曲线
         流进温热的盐海中。
勇敢的群星，
         在眨眼俯视我之前
         留意着高飞的云雀。
看看西风怎样
呼唤云雀去赶赴这无常的约会——
         如此坚信只有他那冰冷的呼吸可以支持她
         可云雀将选择爱
            而不是沉寂。

Nobody's Sugar Daddy Now
David Meischen

The radio was playing Hank Williams when
they found him, steam hissing from the engine
like dancehall smoke beneath the freeway lights.
He got his first car at 16, took to driving west
from town, a hundred miles an hour across
coastal flatland straight into summer's
five o'clock sun, tires beneath him skimming
a shimmer of watery silver, his laughter buffeted
by hot wind whipping through open windows
as field hands turned from the harvest
to shake their heads. Got pummeled
by a jealous rival once, skull bones split
beneath the left eye, laughed when the doctors said
stay on your back, give the bruising
time to ebb, let the skull bones mesh again, or risk
blindness. Sneaked out for a drink instead, shot
a game of pool when the ache beating
beneath narcotic numbness gave way
to nicotine's whispered promise, bourbon's
buttery warmth. Didn't imagine he'd make it
to forty, riding a trajectory that felt pre-
determined—from his grandfather's razor
to the burst of blood inside his father's head—
final as a kiss of skull bones against carframe,
indifferent as the old oak tree biding its time
along a farmroad north of San Antonio,
and year's later, his own son asleep
at the wheel, un-seatbelted like his father,
like his father perhaps dreaming something
gentler than the brunt of bumper against hardwood,
the instant of flight, the sudden darkening.

现在落单的甜爹

大卫·麦森

当人们找到他时，收音机里正播放着
"汉克·威廉姆斯"，发动机还在嘶嘶冒气
就像是高速公路路灯下舞厅里的烟雾。
他十六岁那年获得第一辆车，从小镇出发向西
驶去，以每小时100哩的速度穿过
海边平地直奔向夏日五时的太阳，
他下方的轮胎掠过波光粼粼的水面，
他的笑声乘着热风冲出打开的车窗，
就好像田间劳动者厌恶了收获，
转而摇摇头。一度遭到满怀嫉妒的
对手的打击，左眼下的头骨
裂开，当医生笑着嘱咐他
躺下休息，让身上的伤口有足够的时间
恢复，并让头骨重新愈合，否则就有
失明的危险。他反而溜出去喝酒，玩一把
台球，就在麻痹人的麻木感下生出的剧疼
让位于尼古丁喃喃道出的诺言，波旁威士忌
油腻的热度的时候。
从没想过
他能挨到四十岁，沿着炮弹的曲线，好像早已注定——
从他祖父的剃须刀.
到他父亲脑血管的迸裂——
最后他靠着车框死去，
亲人们留下了一个吻，
就像圣安东尼奥北面乡间小道上的
老橡树一样冷漠，
多年之后，他自己的儿子出车祸死了
原因是像他父亲一样没有系安全带，
也许像他父亲一样会梦见
比保险杠撞击硬木轻柔些的撞击
飞翔的瞬间，突至的黑暗。

a section from
Games
Alysa Hayes

Like a corpse, I hold still.
My breath fills up the space
of silence. In the darkness
I am all body. Dirty shirts
crush and shift below me,
but I'll come clean again.
Light slips through the edges
of the hamper. I see
the other side – the handle
waiting, numb and unpolished,
white paint peeling back
along the bottom ledge.
Here I am, one leg cramping up
beneath me, the other rubbing raw
against wood. My arms are clay
I pour into – palm to lips,
knuckle to brow. Not breathing.
Not breathing. Set like stone,
I cannot come apart.
He will not find me here.

节选自《游戏》

艾莉莎·海斯

如尸体般，我一动不动，
我的呼吸充满了这寂静的
空间。黑暗中的我
整个儿是身体。脏衣服
在我身下被挤压挪移，
但我将会再次和盘托出。
光线从木盒的边缘
悄悄地溜进来。我看到了
另一边——把手
等待着，麻木且粗糙，
白漆沿着底部的架子
向后脱落。
我就在这儿，一条腿盘曲在
身下，另一条被木盒磨得
生疼。我的手臂像黏土一样
我缩成一团——掌心贴着嘴唇，
指节紧靠眉毛。屏息。
屏息。我不能放松，
像石头那样纹丝不动。
他在这里找不到我。

Dust Storm
Larry Thomas

The West Texas sky
at high noon,
turning to nothing
but loose red land
one with wind.
The horses,
looming in the pasture

like bodies
of the drowned
suspended in fathoms
of swirling,
blood-colored earth,
each horse a monument
of composure

tilting a back hoof
in perfect calm
though slowly
being buried alive,
turning to dust
right before the eyes
of the rider.

沙尘暴

赖里·托马斯

正午
德克萨斯西部的天空，
目空一切
只面向疏松的红土地
刮着风的土地。
马匹
在牧场上若隐若现

如溺死的
尸体
悬浮在
漩涡的深渊里
血色的尘土中，
一匹马是一座
镇静的纪念碑。

抬起后蹄
绝对镇定
尽管缓缓地
被活活掩埋，
就在骑手的
眼皮底下
变为尘埃。

Translations

李森 **Li Sen,** 龙晓滢 **Long Xiaoying,** 王浩 **Wang Hao, and** 张晓红 **Zhang Xiaohong:** "Single Cirrus," Wendy Barker • 《孤云》，温迪·巴克 • "Thunder," Wendy Barker • 《雷鸣》，温迪·巴克 • "Quixote," Steven Schroeder • 《堂吉诃德》，史蒂文·施罗德 • "For Some Reason," Nathan Brown • 《因故》，内森·布朗 • "This Alien Place Called Home," James Hoggard • 《这个叫作家的鬼地方》，詹姆斯·霍葛德 • "The Family Secret," Natasha Marin • 《家庭秘密》，娜塔莎·马林 • "Anniversary Trip," James Hoggard • 《周年纪念的旅程》，詹姆斯·霍葛德 • "Burn," Nathan Brown • 《燃烧》，内森·布朗 • "A Note of Thanks," Nathan Brown • 《道谢便条》，内森·布朗 • "Dry Spell," David Meischen • 《干旱期》，大卫·麦森 • "Red-tailed Hawk," James Hoggard • 《红尾鹰》，詹姆斯·霍葛德 • "Mockingbird," Larry Thomas • 《水蒲苇莺》，赖里·托马 • "Condensation Nuclei," Wendy Barker • 《致密的核》，温迪·巴克 • "Windmills," Sherry Craven • 《风车》，雪莉·克莱文 • "a nightingale risks," Natasha Marin • 《夜莺冒险》，娜塔莎·马林 • "Holy is a fragile thing...," Sherry Craven • 《神圣是个纤弱的东西……》，雪莉·克莱文 • "Grace Strokes," Kenneth Hada • 《优雅地划桨》，肯尼斯·哈达 • "Mirage," David Meischen • 《海市蜃楼》，大卫·麦森 • "Gift," Alysa Hayes • 《礼物》，艾莉莎·海斯 • "Blue in the Middle of a Corn Field," Alysa Hayes • 《玉米地里的忧伤》，艾莉莎·海斯 • "The Last Laugh," Alan Berecka • 《最后一笑》，艾伦·巴拉克 • "Renovations at the Santuario de Guadalupe," Nathan Brown • 《翻新德瓜达卢佩圣殿》，内森·布朗 • "Onion Creek, Fall," David Meischen • 《洋葱河》，秋天，大卫·麦森 • "train in the desert at night," Steven Schroeder • 《行驶在沙漠夜色中的列车》，史蒂文·施罗德 • "Pastoral," Alysa Hayes • 《田园》，艾莉莎·海斯 • "Blue Norther," Larry Thomas • 《蓝色北风》，赖里·托马斯 • "prevailing time," Steven Schroeder • 《盛行的时令》，史蒂文·施罗德 • "Low Pressure," Patricia Goodrich • 《低压》，帕特丽夏·古德里奇 • "Woody Guthrie Memorial Highway," Steven Schroeder • 《树木茂密的高斯里公路》，史蒂文·施罗德 • "almost human," Steven Schroeder • 《近乎人类》，史蒂文·施罗德 • "Full Moon, Cirrocumulus, Light Breeze, and Iridescence," Wendy Barker • 《满月、卷积云、清风和虹彩》，温迪·巴克 • "Winter Wedding," Alan Berecka • 《冬日婚礼》，艾伦·巴拉克 • "Near-Earth Object," Wendy Barker • 《临近地球的物体》，温迪·巴克 • "Harvest Moon," Larry Thomas • 《满月》，赖里·托马斯 • "Kite Flying," Sherry Craven • 《断线的风筝》，雪莉·克莱文 • "Nobody's Sugar Daddy

Now," David Meischen • 《现在落单的甜爹》, 大卫·麦森 • a section from "Games," Alysa Hayes • 节选自《游戏》, 艾莉莎·海斯 • "Yu's Wife," Natasha Marin • 《禹的妻子》, 娜塔莎·马林 • "Dust Storm," Larry Thomas • 《沙尘暴》, 赖里·托马斯

李森 Li Sen, 王浩 Wang Hao, 张晓红 Zhang Xiaohong, and 宇丽娟 Zi Lijuan: "La Vida Nada," Jerry Bradley • 《虚空的生活》, 杰里·布拉得雷 • "In Celebration of Gray," Scott Wiggerman • 《庆祝灰色》, 司各特·威格曼 • "September," Scott Wiggerman • 《九月》, 司各特·威格曼 • "October Revival in Texas," Scott Wiggerman • 《德克萨斯十月的复活》, 司各特·威格曼 • "Afterward," Jerry Bradley • 《之后》, 杰里·布拉得雷 • "December," Aaron Rudolph • 《十二月》, 阿龙·鲁道夫 • "Beyond the Entropy of Gophers," Jerry Craven • 《地鼠的混沌之外》, 杰里·克莱文 • "Before the Coming of the Crow," Jerry Craven • 《乌鸦来临之前》, 杰里·克莱文 • "Spring in Palo Duro Canyon," Jerry Craven • 《帕罗杜若峡谷的春天》, 杰里·克莱文 • "The Acuña Brothers Look North, 1952," Aaron Rudolph • 《阿库纳弟兄看北方, 1952 年》, 阿龙·鲁道夫 • "Midsummer Farewell," Jerry Craven • 《仲夏之别》, 杰里·克莱文 • "A Single Sheep, One Cow," Jerry Bradley • 《一只绵羊, 一头牛》, 杰里·布拉得雷 • "Downtown Albuquerque," Aaron Rudolph • 《爱伯克奇市中心》, 阿龙·鲁道夫 • "West of Fort Worth," Scott Wiggerman • 《沃斯城堡以西》, 司各特·威格曼 • "Cleaving a Valentine," Jerry Bradley • 《情人节的断肠人》, 杰里·布拉得雷

张晓红 Zhang Xiaohong and Steven Schroeder 史蒂文·施罗德: 《故事和鸟群》, 海男 • "stories and flocks of birds," Hai Nan • 《身体》, 翟永明 • "bodies," Zhai Yongming • 《在古代》, 翟永明 • "in ancient time," Zhai Yongming • 《面对镜子》, 海男 • "face to face with the mirror," Hai Nan • 《读李后主词仿十四行诗》, 何小竹 • "in the manner of a sonnet, on reading lyric verse by Li Yu, last monarch of Southern Tang," He Xiaozhu • 《他们骂弯了清晨一米》, 唐丹鸿 • "they shout abuses till early morning bends one meter," Tang Danhong • 《梦见苹果和鱼的安》, 何小竹 • "dream of apples and fish," He Xiaozhu • 《鸟群的声音》, 海男 • "the flock's voice," Hai Nan • 《蝴蝶是怎样变成标本的》, 海男 • "how a butterfly becomes a specimen," Hai Nan • 《漂亮的奴隶》, 海男 • "a pretty slave," Hai Nan • 《送一颗炮弹到喜玛拉雅山顶》, 何小竹 • "shoot a bomb to the top of the Himalayas," He Xiaozhu • 《躺在三天宽的歌喉上》, 唐丹鸿 • "lie down on a voice singing three days wide," Tang

Danhong • 《这一天》，吉木朗格 • "this day," Jimu Langge • 《花儿》，唐丹鸿 • "bloom," Tang Danhong • 《五十年代的语言》，瞿永明 • "1950s language," Zhai Yongming • 《阿根廷蚂蚁》，吉木朗格 • "Argentine ants," Jimu Langge • 《押韵是有瘾的》，吉木朗格 • "rhyming is addictive," Jimu Langge • 《不是一头牛，而是一群牛》，何小竹 • "not one head of cattle, but a herd of cattle," He Xiaozhu • 《机关枪新娘》，唐丹鸿 • "machine gun bride," Tang Danhong • 《爱情和马》，吉木朗格 • "love and horse," Jimu Langge • 《重阳登高》，瞿永明 • "mountain climbing on double nine day," Zhai Yongming • 《色达草原》，何小竹 • "Seda Prairie," He Xiaozhu • 《西昌的月亮》，吉木朗格 • "Xichang moon," Jimu Langge • 《当天晚上》，海男 • "that night," Hai Nan • 《虚构的玫瑰》，海男 • "illusive roses," Hai Nan • 《干燥的南部山冈》，海男 • "dry, dry Southern Hills," Hai Nan

王浩 **Wang Hao and Steven Schroeder** 史蒂文 · 施罗德: 《动荡不安的树叶》，李森 • "turbulent leaves," Li Sen • 《内衣的谜诀》，海男 • "the riddle of lingerie," Hai Nan • 《坟墓》，李森 • "grave," Li Sen • 《贪婪》，海男 • "greed," Hai Nan • 《声音和羽毛》，李森 • "sounds and feathers," Li Sen • 《鸟禽畜牲都好歌》，李森 • "song for the good birds and beasts," Li Sen • 《玻璃的味道》，海男 • "the flavor of glass," Hai Nan • 《私秘中的露台》，海男 • "private balcony," Hai Nan • 《昆明的玫瑰》，李森 • "Kunming roses," Li Sen • 《庭院》，李森 • "courtyard," Li Sen • 《红土高原》，李森 • "red earth plateau," Li Sen • 《到底是谁出卖了我》，海男 • "who sold me out in the end?" Hai Nan

梁慧春 **Liang Huichun and Steven Schroeder** 史蒂文 · 施罗德: 《我去过许多地方……》，李南 • "I have been in many places……," Li Nan • 《时光》，李南 • "time," Li Nan • 《甘蔗林》，杨晓芸 • "sugarcane forest," Yang Xiaoyun • 《梦见一个死于车祸的朋友》，刘春 • "dream of a friend who died in a car accident," Liu Chun • 《回故里》，杨晓芸 • "going back to the old neighborhood," Yang Xiaoyun • 《故乡》，李南 • "Hometown," Li Nan • 《打开诗篇》，李南 • "break open psalms," Li Nan • 《我写下的都是卑微的事物》，刘春 • "all I write about are insignificant things," Liu Chun • 《我就将爱上五月》，黄芳 • "I will fall in love with May," Huang Fang • 《遥寄江南》，李南 • "mail from the southern reaches of the Yangtze," Li Nan • 《在广阔的世界上》，李南 • "in the wide world," Li Nan • 《疼》，李南 • "it hurts," Li Nan • 《卡夫卡》，刘春 • "Kafka," Liu Chun • 《瓦蓝瓦蓝的天空》，李南 • "pastel blue sky," Li Nan • 《平安

夜》，黄芳 • "Christmas Eve," Huang Fang • 《桃花》，杨晓芸 • "peach blossom," Yang Xiaoyun • 《毛妹，店》，冉仲景 • "Mao Mei, shop," Ran Zhongjing • 《仿佛这忧伤》，黄芳 • "as if this sadness, were real," Huang Fang

梁慧春 Liang Huichun, 宋子江 Song Zijiang, and Steven Schroeder 史蒂文·施罗德: 《等待》，冉仲景 • "waiting," Ran Zhongjing • 《那些花》，杨晓芸 • "those flowers," Yang Xiaoyun • 《夸耀》，冉仲景 • "exaltation," Ran Zhongjing • 《摆手舞曲：春天》，冉仲景 • "hand-waving dance: spring," Ran Zhongjing • 《减法》，冉仲景 • "subtraction," Ran Zhongjing

何录容 He Lurong, 梁慧春 Liang Huichun, 宋子江 Song Zijiang, and Steven Schroeder 史蒂文·施罗德: 《债务》，冉仲景 • "debt," Ran Zhongjing

梁慧春 Liang Huichun, 宋子江 Song Zijiang, and 张晓红 Zhang Xiaohong: "Drink Water," Patricia Goodrich • 《饮水》，帕特丽夏·古德里奇 • "Our Lady," Patricia Goodrich • 《我们的圣女》，帕特丽夏·古德里奇 • "That Which Clings," Kenneth Hada • 《那紧缠的》，肯尼斯·哈达

Acknowledgments

"Condensation Nuclei," Wendy Barker (《致密的核》，温迪·巴克) first appeared in the *Hollins Critic*. "Full Moon, Cirrocumulus, Light Breeze, and Iridescence," Wendy Barker (《满月、卷积云、清风和虹彩》，温迪·巴克) first appeared in *Chariton Review*. "Near-Earth Object," Wendy Barker (《临近地球的物体》，温迪·巴克) first appeared in *Blue Mesa Review*. "Thunder," Wendy Barker (《雷鸣》，温迪·巴克) first appeared in *Poetry*.

"A Note of Thanks," Nathan Brown (《道谢便条》，内森·布朗); "Burn," Nathan Brown (《燃烧》，内森·布朗); "For Some Reason," Nathan Brown (《因故》，内森·布朗); and "Renovations at the Santuario de Guadalupe," Nathan Brown (《翻新德瓜达卢佩圣殿》，内森·布朗) all appeared in *Ashes Over the Southwest* (Greystone Press, 2005).

"Before the Coming of the Crow," Jerry Craven (《乌鸦来临之前》，杰里·克莱文) appeared in *Sulphur River Review*. "Midsummer Farewell," Jerry Craven (《仲夏之别》，杰里·克莱文) and "Spring in Palo Duro Canyon," Jerry Craven (《帕罗杜若峡谷的春天》，杰里·克莱文) appeared in *Poetry in Texas: a 150 Year Anthology* (ALE Press, 1995).

"Kite Flying," Sherry Craven (《断线的风筝》，雪莉·克莱文) appeared in *Langdon Review of the Arts in Texas*.

"Grace Strokes," Kenneth Hada (《优雅地划桨》，肯尼斯·哈达) appeared in *The Way of the Wind* (Village Books Press, 2008). "That Which Clings," Kenneth Hada (《那紧缠的》，肯尼斯·哈达) appeared in *Poesia* and in *The Way of the Wind* (Village Books Press, 2008).

《漂亮的奴隶》，海男 ("a pretty slave," Hai Nan); 《干燥的南部山冈》，海男 ("dry, dry southern hills," Hai Nan); 《面对镜子》，海男 ("face to face with the mirror," Hai Nan); 《蝴蝶是怎样变成标本的》，海男 ("how a butterfly becomes a specimen," Hai Nan); 《虚构的玫瑰》，海男 ("illusive roses," Hai Nan); 《当天晚上》，海男 ("that night," Hai Nan); and 《鸟群的声音》，海男 ("the flock's voice," Hai Nan) appeared in *The Secret of Flight* (Virtual Artists Collective, 2004).

"Anniversary Trip," James Hoggard (《周年纪念的旅程》, 詹姆斯·霍葛德) appeared in *Medea In Taos* (San Antonio: Pecan Grove Press, 2000). "Red-tailed Hawk," James Hoggard (《红尾鹰》, 詹姆斯·霍葛德) appeared in *Wearing The River: New Poems* (San Antonio: Wings Press, 2005).

《故乡》, 李南 ("hometown," Li Nan) and 《瓦蓝瓦蓝的天空》, 李南 ("pastel blue sky," Li Nan) appeared in *Small/ 小* (Virtual Artists Collective, 2007). 《我去过许多地方……》, 李南 ("I have been in many places……," Li Nan); 《在广阔的世界上》, 李南 ("in the wide world," Li Nan) appeared in *Small/ 小* (Virtual Artists Collective, 2007) and in *the drunken boat*.

"almost human," Steven Schroeder (《近乎人类》, 史蒂文·施罗德) appeared in *Mid-America Poetry Review*. "Quixote," Steven Schroeder (《堂吉诃德》, 史蒂文·施罗德) and "Woody Guthrie Memorial Highway," Steven Schroeder (《树木茂密的高斯里公路》, 史蒂文·施罗德) appeared online at steven-schroeder.blogspot.com.

"Blue Norther," Larry Thomas (《蓝色北风》, 赖里·托马斯) appeared in *Southwestern American Literature* and *Where Skulls Speak Wind* (Texas Review Press, 2004). "Dust Storm," Larry Thomas (《沙尘暴》, 赖里·托马斯) appeared in *The Cape Rock* and *Amazing Grace* (Texas Review Press, 2001). "Harvest Moon," Larry Thomas (《满月》, 赖里·托马斯) appeared in *The Texas Observer* and *Stark Beauty* (Timberline Press, 2005). "Mockingbird," Larry Thomas (《水蒲苇莺》, 赖里·托马斯) appeared in *REAL: Regarding Arts & Letters* and in *Amazing Grace* (Texas Review Press, 2001).

Cover photo and photos on pages 10, 34, and 194 by Chen Chuan.

Title page photo and photo on page 90 by Herbert Schroeder.

Photo on page 41 by Jerry Craven.

Photos on pages 116 and 240 by Zhang Dongdong.

Photo on page 246 by David Meischen.

Photos on pages 16 and 191 by Steven Schroeder.

Afterword: On *Two Southwests*

Under the influence of one way of thinking about science, we in "the West" have tended to act as though the more we can distance ourselves emotionally, the better we can see. From the bottom of my heart, I disagree. In the argument between Newton and Goethe about what happens in color vision, I side with Goethe: the world is a place made of edges – and edges, what we make of them, what they make of us, are as important as what light does or does not contain in making color happen.

In the argument between Newton and Newton, I side with the alchemist: there is magic in the ordinary that makes the extraordinary possible.

Paradoxically, the privileging of distance under the name of objectivity has often diverted attention from the concrete present of an object to the abstract absence of it. *Be objective* stands in for *objectify*. But I am convinced that we see and know most fully what touches us most deeply. And, whatever else you may say about touching and being touched deeply, it is, indisputably, a matter of bodies coming into contact. It is a matter of collision – who meets whom how where when.

Hence this project – "two southwests," two variations on an illusion of geographic precision behind which there are people who find themselves in both *natural* environments and *political* ones, who come to know in various ways that what we can and cannot see is as likely to depend on a map as a mountain – or when and where the river is dry enough to cross. What we say and what we don't, as surely as what we see and what we can't, are products of politics as well as location. But, politics and perspective aside, it is a matter of collision – and putting ourselves in places where we will collide can be an aid to vision.

This project, by bringing poets and other artists together in two places similarly named by virtue of their respective places on somebody else's maps, is intended to facilitate a collision. And the shape it takes is a matter of chance encounters as well as of circles of friends. We call it "two southwests," but these southwests revolve around Texas and Yunnan at least in part because the friends who initiated it (brought together by another friend) each identify by origin with one of those places. We have gathered circles for this project starting where we are. Where else?

241

Poets and visual artists (as well as musicians and translators) are typically as interested in what is not there as in what is. There is some controversy about this, of course, among both artists and critics. But it has been my experience that the best translators, like the best teachers, are those who have the patience for silence. And my attraction to "Eastern" aesthetics may have something to do with the recognition in much of the tradition that "empty" space on paper or canvas is as important to a picture as space that is "full." But I think it also has to do with growing up in a place where there is clearly nothing to see. In our southwests, there is space for silence – and the intersection of sky with earth on open plains can teach you to appreciate nothing whether the plateau beneath your feet is below Tibet or above the Caprock.

This *between* is worth exploring – especially as it connects to the collisions of bodies that give us an experience of touching and being touched. Our hope is that the *betweenness* will be illuminated by setting images side by side: between the pictures we may hear silence; between the poems and between the lines nothing that is there may make our being present a bit more possible.

Steven Schroeder
July 2008
Chicago, Illinois

后 记
——关于《两个西南》

史蒂文·施罗德

在科学式的单线思维的影响下，我们这些"西部"人似乎一直以为情感距离越大，我们看得就越清楚。我打心底里不同意这种看法。就牛顿和歌德关于色彩视觉的争论而言，我站在歌德这边：世界是由边际构成的；不论我们如何看待边际，边际如何造就我们，边际之重要，不亚于光对色彩构成的重要性。

对于牛顿与牛顿之间的争论，我与作为炼金术士的牛顿站在一边：平凡的事物中存在着造就不平凡事物的魔力。

奇怪的是，以客观性为由大谈距离，往往把我们的注意力从事物具体的当下转向它抽象的缺席。"保持客观"取代了"客观性"。但是我相信，我们看得最清楚，了解最深刻的，是那些深深打动我们的事物。不论您对深深打动别人还是被别人深深打动有些什么样的看法，毫无疑问，它指的是身体的接触，是一种冲撞，即谁在何时、何地、如何遇上他人。

"两个西南"项目由是而生。这是对地域上的精确性产生的两种幻象，在这种幻象之后，人们既处于自然环境之中，也处于政治环境之中；他们以不同的方式认识到，我们所能看到和不能看到的东西，既依赖于地图也依赖于山峰，或者说河流在何时、何地干涸得足以让我们跨越。我们所说和不说的，确切如我们能看到的和不能看到的，都是政治和地理位置的产物。政治和视角且不论，关键在于冲撞，将我们置身于发生冲撞的地方可能有助于拓展我们的视野。

这个项目把来自两个地方——它们由于在别人地图上所处的位置而具有相似的称谓——的诗人和其他艺术家汇聚到一起，其目的在于引发一种冲撞。这个项目的形式则是由朋友圈子和意外的邂逅造就的。我们将其称作"两个西南"，但这些西南地区多少以德克萨斯和云南为中心，这是因为发起这个项目的朋友们（一个朋友带来另一个朋友）均来自其中的一个地方。我们为这个项目招集友人——从我们所在的地方开始。不从这里，又从哪里呢？

诗人和视觉艺术家（还有音乐家和翻译家）对在场的事物和不在场的事物都特别感兴趣。当然，无论是艺术家还是批评家对此都颇有争议。但是根据我的经验，最优秀的翻译家就像最优秀的教师一样，是那些对沉默有耐心的人。我之所以被"东方"美学吸引，可能出自对"飞白"这一传统的肯定——纸张和画布上的"空"与图画中的"满"不分轩轾。但我想这也是因为我生长在一个"无物可看"的地方。我们的西南地区，有着留给沉默的空间，空旷平原上的天地相交之处，教人学会如何去欣赏"无"，而不论脚下的高原是在西藏之下还是开普洛克之上。

"在……之间"这个词值得探究，因为它涉及身体的冲撞，而这种冲撞又给予我们触动他人和被他人触动的经验。我们希望通过把各种形象并列在一起，从而说明这种"之间"的涵义；在诗歌之间，在诗句之间，"不存在的事物"可以使我们的当下进一步成为可能。

Contributors

Wendy Barker has published four books of poetry and two chapbooks. She has twice received the Violet Crown Book Award (for *Way of Whiteness*, Wings Press, 2000, and for *Between Frames*, Pecan Grove Press, 2006). Other awards include the Sourette Diehl Fraser award for her translations (with Saranindranath Tagore), *Rabindranath Tagore: Final Poems* (Braziller, 2001), an NEA fellowship, and a Rockefeller fellowship to Bellagio. Her poems have appeared in such journals as *The American Scholar*, *Poetry*, and *Gettysburg Review*, and she has new work forthcoming from *Georgia Review*, *Mid-American Review*, and *Marlboro Review*. She is Poet in Residence and a professor of English at the University of Texas at San Antonio.

温迪•巴克的第三本诗集《白路》（翅膀出版社2000，2004）和《火焰之间》（山核桃林出版社，2006）获得紫罗兰冠图书奖。和萨拉宁德兰纳斯•泰戈尔合作翻译的诗集《拉宾德兰纳斯•泰戈尔：最后的诗歌》（布拉斯勒出版社2001），并获得了有德克萨斯文学研究所颁发的索勒•狄赫•弗拉塞奖，也曾获得美国国家艺术捐赠会奖金和贝亚乔洛克菲勒奖金。其诗歌曾在《美国学者》、《诗歌》和《吉蒂斯博格评论》发表，将会在《乔治亚评论》、《美国中部评论》和《马尔博罗评论》，被翻译成印度语，日语和保加利亚语。温迪•巴克是一位驻留诗人和英语教授，任教于圣安东尼奥市的德克萨斯大学。

Alan Berecka is a reference librarian at Del Mar College in Corpus Christi, Texas. His poetry has appeared in *American Literary Review, Texas Review, Ardent, Windhover, Slow Trains, Christian Century*, and *Red River Review*. His chapbook, *Each Man Has One Life*, was published by Trilobite Press in 2004.

艾伦•巴拉克在位于德克萨斯州科博斯克里斯蒂市的德尔玛学院担任参考馆员。其诗刊登在《美国文艺评论》、《德克萨斯评论》、《热心》、《缓慢列车》、《基督世纪》和《红河评论》。他的诗歌小册子《一人一命》由特里洛拜特出版社于2004年出版。

Jerry Bradley is Professor of English at Lamar University. He is the author of four books, including *The Movement: British Poets of the 1950s* (Twayne) and a collection of poetry entitled *Simple Versions of Disaster* (University of North Texas Press), which was commended by the *Dictionary of Literary Biography*. His poetry has appeared in many literary magazines, including *New England Review, American Literary Review, Modern Poetry Studies, Poetry Magazine*, and *Southern Humanities Review*. He is also Poetry Editor of *Concho River Review* and is Past-President of the Texas Association of

Creative Writing Teachers and of the Southwest/Texas Popular Culture Association.

杰里•布拉德雷是拉玛尔大学研究生课程主任也是该大学的研究会副主席。目前著作四本，其中包括《那场运动：1950 年代的英国诗人》（特温出版社）和《灾难的简版》（北德克萨斯州大学出版社），被收录进《文艺传记词典》。其诗歌刊登在很多文艺杂志上，包括《新英格兰评论》、《美国文艺评论》、《现代诗歌研究》、《诗歌杂志》和《南方人文评论》。曾在德克萨斯创作教师协会和西南/德克萨斯流行文化协会担任主席，现今在《乡河评论》担任诗歌编辑。

Nathan Brown has published five collections of poetry: *Hobson's Choice, Ashes Over the Southwest, Suffer the Little Voices* (a finalist for the 2006 Oklahoma Book Award), *Not Exactly Job*, and *Two Tables Over*. He worked as a professional songwriter and musician for more than fifteen years in and around Oklahoma City, Nashville, and Austin. He has also performed in Israel and Russia, and worked with artists like Cynthia Clawson, Billy Crockett, and Tom Wopat. He has recorded five of his own albums. The two most recent are "Why in the Road" and "Driftin' Away." Nathan holds an interdisciplinary Ph.D. in English and Journalism from the University of Oklahoma. He teaches for the Human Relations and Liberal Studies departments at the University of Oklahoma and has also served as the Artist-in-Residence at the University of Central Oklahoma.

内森•布朗出版的 5 本诗集为《霍布森的选择》、《西南的灰烬》、《小声音的折磨》（此诗集入围 2006 年奥克拉荷马图书奖的最后名单）、《并非完全是工作》和《那边的两张桌子》。作为拥有 15 年经验的专业歌曲家和音乐家，活跃于奥克拉荷马城，纳什维尔和奥斯丁及其周边地区，也曾在以色列和俄罗斯进行演奏，并和多位艺术家合作，包括苹提亚•克劳森、比利•克罗克特和汤姆•沃帕特。录制了属于自己的 5 个专辑，最近录制的两个专辑为《为什么在路上》和《德里夫廷的离开》。内森从奥克拉荷马大学修得英语和新闻学的跨学科博士学位，现在任教于该大学的人文学系和人际关系学系也是现任的奥克拉荷马中心大学的驻校艺术家。

Jerry Craven, a native Texan, publishes poetry, fiction, creative nonfiction, and books for children. He has taught for five universities in three countries and has lived for extended periods of time in Asia, the Middle East, Europe, and South America. He has published 20 books including *Tickling Catfish, a Texan Looks at Culture from Amarillo to Borneo* (creative nonfiction), *Snake Mountain* (a novel), and three collections of poetry. Currently he lives on the edge of the Angelina National Forest in Texas and commutes to Lamar University where he is Visiting Writer in Residence.

杰里·克莱文是土生土长的德克萨斯人。出版作品有诗歌、小说、创作性散文和儿童读物。曾在三个国家的五间大学任教,并在亚洲、中东、欧洲和南美都生活了较长的时间。出版的20本书包括《惹痒的鲶鱼》、《一本德克萨斯的书:从阿玛利约到博尔内奥的文化》(创作性散文)、《蛇山》(小说)和三本诗集。现今在拉玛尔大学作为驻校访问作家并生活在德克萨斯州的安吉丽娜国家森林的边缘,常常往返两地。

Sherry Craven taught English and creative writing at Midland College in Midland, Texas for eleven years and taught in the English Department at West Texas A&M University. She has published poetry in both English and Spanish in various literary journals and read her work at numerous writers conferences and for NPR radio.

雪梨•克莱文曾在德克萨斯州的米德兰德学院教授英语和创作达11年,也曾任教于西德克萨斯A&M大学的英语系。其创作的英语和西班牙语诗歌在多种文艺刊物上发表,她曾多次在作家会议和全美公共广播电台朗诵自己的诗作。

Patricia Goodrich is a writer and visual artist. Goodrich's work is published and exhibited in the Federation of Russia, Lithuania, Romania and Turkey, as well as in the USA. She has six collections of poetry and has been awarded Pennsylvania Fellowships in Poetry and Creative Nonfiction.

帕特丽夏·古德里奇,作家,视觉艺术家。其作品在俄罗斯联邦、立陶宛、罗马尼亚、土耳其和美国等多个国家出版和展出。已出版六本诗集,曾获得宾夕法尼亚诗歌与创作性散文奖金。

Kenneth Hada is an Associate Professor in the English Department at East Central University in Ada, Oklahoma. Some of his poetry appears in his recent book, *The Way of the Wind* (Village Books Press), as well as in *Oklahoma Today, Poesia, RE:AL, Flint Hills Review, Crosstimbers, Westview, Kansas City Voices,* among others. He also directs the annual Scissortail Creative Writing Festival held the first weekend of each April on the campus of ECU.

肯尼斯·哈达奥克拉荷马州阿达市东部中心大学英语系副教授。近来,其诗歌发表于《风路》(村野之书出版社),刊登于《今日奥克拉荷马》、《诗艺》、《RE:AL》、《弗林特众山评论》、《跨木》、《西部评论》、《肯萨斯城市声音》等杂志。每年四月的第一个周末他都在东部加州大学校园主持年度"铁尾鸟创作节"。

海男，1962 年出生于中国云南，是位多产诗人。出版了四本中文诗集，包括《风琴与女人》（1992），《虚构的玫瑰》（1995），《是什么在背后》（1997），《唇色》（2001）。另外，海男也至少出版了 15 本小说。

Hai Nan was born in 1962 in Yunnan, People's Republic of China. A prolific poet, she has published four poetry collections in Chinese: *Organ and Woman* (1992), *Illusive Roses* (1995), *What Lies Behind* (1997), and *The Color of Lips* (2001). Hai Nan has also published more than fifteen novels.

Alysa Hayes received a BA from Texas A&M University, where she won the 2005 Gordone Award in Poetry. She is published in *Callaloo*, and teaches creative arts classes with Theater Action Project (TAP) in Austin, Texas.

艾丽莎·海斯，获德克萨斯州A&M大学学士学位，并获得2005年该校格尔顿诗歌奖。在《卡亚鲁》发表诗歌，目前在德克萨斯州奥斯丁市的"剧场行动项目"教授创意艺术课程。

何录容，1983 年出生于湖南郴州。于泰山学院获得学士学位。现在在深圳大学修读英语文学的研究生课程。

He Lurong, born in 1983 in Chenzhou, Hunan. After getting B.A. in Taishan College, she is now a postgraduate majoring in English Literature in Shenzhen University.

何小竹出生于四川省的一个苗族家庭。在 20 世纪 80 年代作为非非主义诗人参与了第三代诗歌运动。出版的三本诗集为《梦见苹果和鱼的安》、《回头的羊》、《6 个动词，或苹果》。

He Xiaozhu was born into a Miao ethnic family in Sichuan province. He participated in "the third generation" movement as a member of the "nay-nayist" poetry group in the 1980s. He has published three poetry collections: *Dream of Apples and Fishes, The Sheep Turning Back*, and *Six Verbs or Apples*.

James Hoggard, whose poetry has been praised for its intensity and fine sense of craft, has also won awards and acclaim for his fiction, literary translation, and personal essays. A former NEA fellow and past president of the Texas Institute of Letters, his work has been published throughout the U.S. as well as in Canada, India, England, the Czech Republic, and Cuba. He is the Perkins-Prothro Distinguished Professor of English at Midwestern State University. His most recent collection of poems, *Wearing The River: New Poems*, won the 2007 PEN Southwest Award for Poetry.

詹姆斯·霍莴德，其诗歌强度和诗意之敏锐倍受称誉，其小说、文学翻译和随笔等也获得了多种荣誉和奖项。他曾获得美国国家艺术捐赠会奖金，也曾担任德克萨斯文学研究所所长。其作品在美国、加拿大、印度、英国、捷克共和国和古巴等多个国家出版。拥有佩金斯-普洛夫洛杰出教授的称号，现任教于德克萨斯州维奇塔市中西部州立大学英语系。其最近出版的诗集《以河为衣：新诗》获得2007年度西南诗歌奖。

黄芳，女，生于中国广西贵港。毕业于广西师范大学中文系。曾在《诗刊》、《星星》、《诗选刊》、《诗歌月刊》、《上海文学》、《青年文学》等刊物发表作品。作品入选多种年度选本。获"中国2005年女子诗歌年度奖"。出版诗集《是蓝，是一切》。现就职于桂林某媒体从事记者编辑工作。

Huang Fang was born in Guangxi Guigang. She graduated from the Department of Chinese at Guangxi Normal University. Her work has appeared in *Shi Kan* (*Poetry Journal*), *Xingxing* (*Stars*), *Shi Xuan Kan* (*Selected Poems Journal*), *Shige Yue Kan* (*Poetry Monthly*), *Shanghai Wenxue* (*Shanghai Literature*), *Qingnian Wenxue* (*Youth Literature*), and other publications. Selected works in a variety of anthologies. Winner of the "2005 China's Woman Poet of the Year Prize." Published a collection of poems called is blue, is everything. She now works in Guilin as an editor and reporter.

吉木狼格出生在四川省的一个彝族家庭，于1983开始创作诗歌并作为代表性的非非主义诗人参与了第三代诗歌运动。《怀疑骆驼》、《红狐狸的树》、《睡觉或做梦》、《榜样》和《阴谋》是其最负盛名的几首作品。吉木狼格于2000年开始小说。

Jimu Langge was born into a Yi ethnic family in Sichuan. He began writing poetry in 1983 and participated in "the third generation" poetry movement as a major proponent of "nay-nayism" in the 1980s. "Suspect the Camel," "The Red Fox's Tree," "Sleep or Dream," "Role Model," and "Conspiracy" are among his best-known works. He started writing fiction from 2000 onwards.

李南，1964年出生于中国青海，现定居在河北。1983年开始创作诗歌以来，一共出版了两本诗集。其诗歌被收录进中国多本重要的中文诗歌选集。曾为记者和自由作家。

Li Nan, born in 1964 in Qinghai, People's Republic of China, now lives in Hebei. Since she started writing poetry in 1983, she has published two collections, and her work has been included in important anthologies of Chinese poetry. A former journalist, she is now a freelance writer.

李森，1966 年生于中国云南省腾冲县，1988 年毕业于云南大学并留校任教。现任云南大学艺术与设计学院院长，教授。在《花城》、《作家》、《读书》、《人民文学》等刊物上发表诗歌、散文、学术论文 300 余篇。在中外出版《画布上的影子》（东方出版社 2000 年版）、《我心中的画师》（广西师大出版社 2002 年版）、《动物世说》（花城出版社 2002 年版）、《鸟天下》（中国工人出版社 2004 年版）、《荒诞而迷人的游戏》（学林出版社 2004 年版）、《苍山夜话》（学林出版社 2006 年版）、《中国风车》（美国芝加哥虚拟艺术家合作社 2007 年出版）、《教育的危机》（花城出版社 2008 年版）等 8 部著作，主编《新诗品——昆明芝加哥小组》（与史蒂文·施罗德等合作，云南大学出版社 2008 年版）等刊物和著作 10 余部。是中国著名的"他们"诗派成员之一。

Li Sen was born in 1966 in Tengchong County, Yunnan Province, People's Republic of China. He has been working at Yunnan University since he graduated in 1988. Currently, he is professor and Dean of the School of Art and Design. He has published more than 300 poems, essays, and academic papers in a number of domestic and international magazines and journals, including *Hua Cheng* (Flower City), *Writers*, *Reading*, and *People's Literature*. He has published eight books, including *Shadows on the Canvas* (Dongfang Publishing House, 2000), *Accounts of Animals* (Huacheng Publishing House, 2002), *Painters in My Heart* (Guangxi Normal University Press, 2002), *Birds' World* (China Workers' Publishing House, 2004), *Absurd but Attractive Games* (Xuelin Publishing House, 2004), *Cangshan Night Talk* (Xuelin Publishing House, 2006), *Chinese Windmill* (Virtual Artists Collective, Chicago, USA, 2007), and *Educational Crisis* (Huacheng Publishing House, 2008) . He has edited over ten books, including *New Poetry Appreciation—Kunming-Chicago Group* (in collaboration with Steven Schroeder, Yunnan University Press, 2008). He is one of the poets known as "They," an influential poetry group of China.

梁慧春是马里兰大学的一位中国语言文学讲师。与湛静合作编写《中文成语》。和斯蒂文•施罗德合作翻译李南的诗集《小》。其翻译出现在"透明的语言：多媒体网页词典"、《四川文学》和《犀牛》。其作品刊登在《大公报》（香港），《星岛日报》（美国），也在中国透过众多媒体发表文论。

Liang Huichun is a Lecturer in Chinese language and literature at the University of Maryland. She is the co-author (with Zhanjing) of *Chinese Idioms* and co-translator (with Steven Schroeder) of *Small* (poetry by Li Nan). Her translations have appeared on the Transparent Languages multimedia web pages and dictionary, in *Sichuan Literature*, and *Rhino*; and her writing has appeared in *Da*

Gong (Hong Kong), *Sing Tao Daily* (US), and a variety of media in the People's Republic of China.

刘春，曾用笔名西岩、刘项等。20 世纪 70 年代初期生于广西荔浦县歧路村。在《人民文学》、《诗刊》、《上海文学》、《青年文学》、《星星》、《北京文学》、《天涯》、《南方文坛》、《山花》、《江南》、《芙蓉》等权威文学刊物发表过大量作品，入选过近百种选刊和选本。著有诗集《忧伤的月亮》、《运草车穿过城市》、《幸福像花儿开放》、《刘春卷》，文化随笔集《博尔赫斯的夜晚》、《或明或暗的关系》、《让时间说话》，诗学专著《朦胧诗以后》等；编有《70 后诗歌档案》（上、下册）。获得过诗刊社首届"华文青年诗人奖"、广西人民政府文艺创作最高奖"铜鼓奖"、北京市文艺评论奖、广西文艺评论奖、广西金嗓子青年文学奖等奖项。2000 年创办"扬子鳄"网络诗歌论坛，2002 年参加第 18 届"青春诗会"。现居桂林。为桂林市作家协会副主席。

Liu Chun was born in Lipu County of Guangxi province. His work has appeared in the *People's Literature, Poetry Magazine, Shanghai Literture, Youth Literature, Stars, Beijing Literature, Tianya, Southern Forum, Shanhua, Jiangnan, Furong,* and other literary magazines, as well as hundreds of anthologies. He has published collections such as *Melancholic Moon, The Straw Wagon Went through the City, Happiness Bloomed as Flowers, Liu Chun Volume,* the essay collection *Evening of Borges, Ambiguous Relationship, Let the Time Speak, Poetics After Misty Poetry: the map of the Chinese poetry stage 1986-2007,* etc. He also edited *Poetry Files for the generation after the 70s.* Awarded first "Chinese Youth Poet" prize from *Poetry Magazine,* best award of Bronze Drum by Guangxi People's Government, Beijing City Literary Criticism Award, Guangxi Literary Criticism Award, Guangxi Golden Voice Youth Literary Award, etc. He created "Yangzi Alligator" Poetry Forum, and participated in the 18th "Youth Poetry Conference" in 2002. He is living in Guilin and is the vice president of the Guilin Writers Association.

龙晓滢，云南曲靖人，云南大学中文系文艺学专业在读博士生。部分诗歌翻译发表于《新诗品》（第一卷）（云南大学出版社 2008 年 1 月版）。

Long Xiaoying was born in Qujing, Yunnan Province. She is a doctoral candidate in Literary Theory at Yunnan University. Some of her poetry translations have appeared in *New Poetry Appreciation* (the 1st issue, Yunnan University Press 2008).

Natasha Marin is a conceptual artist and poet living in Austin, Texas. She holds degrees in English from Tufts University and the University of Texas, respectively. She is Cave Canem fellow, an Affrilachian Poet and co-founder of the Gibbous Moon Collective. In 2006, the City of

Austin agreed to co-sponsor her interactive art installation project entitled *Graduate-Level Graffiti* with a cultural arts grant. Her work has appeared in several publications including the *Feminist Studies Journal* and the *South Carolina Review*.

娜塔莎·马林是德克萨斯州奥斯丁市的概念艺术家、诗人。分别在图芙慈大学和德克萨斯大学修读英语并获得学位,为卡文凯侬诗歌奖获得者、阿福里契亚诗人之一、吉博斯月亮团体创办人之一。2006年,奥斯丁市划拨文化艺术创作经费部分资助其名为"研究生涂鸦"的互动式装置艺术项目。其作品发表于《女性主义研究》和《南卡罗莱纳评论》等刊物。

A native of rural South Texas, **David Meischen** has been writing poetry since his mid-thirties. Winner of the Merit Scholarship in Poetry for the Taos Summer Writers' Conference, 2004, he has poems upcoming in *Cider Press Review*. His poetry has appeared in *The Southern Review, Southern Poetry Review, Borderlands, Texas Poetry Journal* and *Di-Verse-City*. Meischen is the co-founder of Dos Gatos Press, non-profit publisher of the *Texas Poetry Calendar*. The proud father of two sons, now in their mid-twenties, he lives in Austin, Texas, with his partner Scott Wiggerman and their cat Silver.

大卫·麦森是土生土长的南德克萨斯人。三十多岁开始写诗歌,并于2004年获得由"塔奥斯夏天作家会议"颁发的诗歌奖金。其诗歌刊登于《南方评论》、《南方诗歌评论》,《边境之地》,《德克萨斯诗刊》和《诗句都市》,并将于近期发表在《苹果汁出版社评论》。麦森是"两只猫"出版社(曾出版《德克萨斯诗歌日历》的一家非营利出版社)的创办人之一。膝下两子二十出头,颇为之自豪。现与同伴斯科特·韦格曼和爱猫"阿银"同住于德克萨斯州奥斯丁市。

冉仲景,男,土家族,1966年生,重庆人。曾参加《诗刊》社第15届青春诗会。出版有诗集《从朗诵到吹奏》。

Ran Zhongjing lives in Chongqing. Participated in the 15th Poetry Magazine Youth Conference. Published a collection of poems called *From Reading to Play*.

Aaron Rudolph has lived most of his life in the American southwest, drawing many of his subjects from the region's people and their long-surviving cultures. His work is as likely to feature burritos and BBQ as it is offer an image of the Sangre de Cristo mountains or a tumbleweed floating along a rural South Plains road. Rudolph is the author of the poetry collection *Sacred Things*.

阿龙·鲁道夫长期生活在美国西南部，其作品多取材于该地区的人和那里源远流长的文化。其作品取材广泛，或是玉米煎饼和烧烤，或是基督之血山脉的景象，或是在南方平原的村路上漂流的风滚草。出有诗集《圣物》。

Steven Schroeder grew up in the Texas Panhandle, where he first learned to take nothing seriously, and his poetry continues to be rooted in the experience of the Plains. His work has appeared or is forthcoming in *Concho River Review*, the *Cresset*, *Druskininkai Poetic Fall 2005*, *Georgetown Review*, *Karamu*, *Mid-America Poetry Review*, *Poetry East*, *Rhino*, *Shichao*, *Sichuan Literature*, *Texas Review*, and other literary journals. His most recent collection is *The Imperfection of the Eye*, published by Virtual Artists Collective in 2007. *Six Stops South* is forthcoming from Cherry Grove Collections.

斯蒂文·施罗德在德克萨斯州的磐瀚德尔长大，并在那里第一次学会了关注虚无。其诗歌从此植根于在平原上的生活经验。他的作品刊登在《金属灯座》、《德鲁斯金宁凯2005秋天诗歌节》、《乔治镇评论》、《卡拉姆》、《美国中部诗歌评论》、《东部诗歌》、《犀牛》、《诗潮》、《四川文学》、《德克萨斯评论》等等众多文艺刊物上。其最近的诗集为《眼的不完美》（虚实艺术家团体2007）。《南方六站》将会在近期出版于"樱桃丛集"。

宋子江，1985年出生于广东，2008年在深圳大学获得英语文学学士学位，现今进修于澳门大学。2005年开始写诗。2007年至今参与澳门故事协会的多个关于诗歌的项目，并和澳大利亚诗人客远文合作翻译诗歌。其参与翻译的宋朝女诗人诗词选集：《采芙蓉》近期将会在澳门故事协会和虚实艺术家团体进行出版。

Song Zijiang was born in 1985 in Guangdong, PRC. He attained BA in English from Shenzhen University and is now studying in the University of Macau. Began writing poems in 2005. Since 2007 he has been participating in poetry-related projects of A.S.M. (Association of Stories in Macao) and co-translating poems with Australian poet Christopher Kelen. The Song Dynasty female poets anthology, *pluck a lotus for pleasure*, which he co-translated, is about to be published by ASM and Virtual Artists Collective.

唐丹鸿，1965年出生于四川成都。毕业于四川大学。曾在华西医药大学担任图书馆员。1994开办卡夫卡书店。1997年开始其独立电视节目制作人和导演。其最负盛名的作品包括《机关枪新娘》和《你躺在三天宽的歌喉上》。

Tang Danhong was born in 1965 in Chengdu and graduated from Sichuan University. She worked as a librarian at Huaxi Medical

University. In 1994 she opened Kafka Bookstore. From 1997 onwards, she began her career as an independent TV producer and director. Her best-known works include "Machine Gun Bride" and "Lie Down on a Voice Singing Three Days Wide."

Larry D. Thomas, born and reared in West Texas, has resided in Houston since 1967. He moved from West Texas to Houston at the age of twenty to complete his college education, and graduated from the University of Houston in 1970 with a BA degree in English literature. In 1998, he retired from a career in adult criminal justice, the last fifteen years of which he served as a branch director for the Harris County Adult Probation Department (Houston). Since his retirement, he has been employed as a full-time poet. His first collection of poetry, *The Lighthouse Keeper*, was published by Timberline Press in late 2000, approximately three years after his retirement, and was selected by the *Small Press Review* as a "pick-of-the-issue" (May/June 2001). He has since that time published six additional collections of poems which have received several prestigious prizes and awards. He has been selected as Poet Laureate of Texas for 2008.

赖利·托马斯,出生于德克萨斯州西部并在当地务农。其 20 岁的时候,即 1967 年,移居休斯顿以完成大学的学业,1970 年在休斯顿大学获得英语 文学学士学位。1983 起担任休斯顿哈里斯镇成人缓刑部主管 15 年,并于 1998 年从成年刑事司法机构退休。退休后潜心创作诗歌,仅仅 3 年后便出 版其第一本诗集《守灯塔的人》(林边出版社 2000),《小出版社评论》 于 2001 年 5 月和 6 月一期称赞该诗集为"此题材之巅峰之作"。其后出版 了 6 本诗集并获得了众多奖项。2008 年被选为德克萨斯桂冠诗人。

王浩,1974 年出生于中国云南,供职于云南大学国际合作与交流处。

Wang Hao was born in 1974 in Yunnan. He works at the Office of International Cooperation and Exchange, Yunnan University.

Scott Wiggerman is the author of *Vegetables and Other Relationships* (Plain View Press, 2000) and editor of the *Texas Poetry Calendar* (Dos Gatos Press), now in its eleventh year. His work has appeared in numerous journals, including *Borderlands, Texas Poetry Review, Poesia, Heartland Review, Midwest Poetry Review, Spillway, Sojourn,* and *the Paterson Literary Review*. In addition, his poems appear in several anthologies, including *This New Breed: Gents, Bad Boys and Barbarians 2* (Windstorm Creative, 2004), *In the Arms of Words: Poems for Disaster Relief* (Sherman Asher, 2006), and *Queer Collection* (Fabulist Flash, 2007).

斯科特·韦格曼是《蔬菜和其它关系》（平原景观出版社 2000）的作者。担任《德克萨斯诗歌日历》（两只猫出版社）的编辑已达十年。其诗歌收入几种文集，包括《这些新品种：绅士、坏男孩、和野蛮人（2）》（风暴创作，2004 年）、《在文字的臂弯里：宽慰灾难的诗歌》（谢尔曼·阿舍尔，2006）和《粉红集》（寓言家之光 2007）。

杨晓芸，女，生于七十年代，从事美术工作，现居四川绵阳。诗歌散见于《诗刊》、《星星诗刊》、《山花》、《诗歌月刊》、《人民文学》、《天涯》等刊物及其它年度选本。

Yang Xiaoyun is an artist who lives in Mianyang, Sichuan Province. Her poetry has appeared in *Shi Kan (Poetry Journal), Xingxing Shikan (Star Poetry Journal), Shanhua, Shige Yuekan (Poetry Monthly), Renmin Wenxue (People's Literature), Tianya,* and other publications.

翟永明，生于四川，毕业于成都电子科技大学。1981 年开始发表诗歌，其完成于 1984 年并于一年后发表的《女人》组诗被称誉为中国女性诗歌的开山之作和试金石。1986 年辞去工作，1990-1991 年在美国生活，1992 年返回成都，1998 年开"白夜酒吧"。其代表作包括《女人》、《称之为一切》、《静安庄》。

Zhai Yongming was born in Sichuan and graduated from Chengdu Telecommunication Engineering College. She began publishing poems in 1981. The poem-series "Woman," which was completed in 1984 and came out one year after, has been acclaimed as the groundbreaking work and touchstone of "women's poetry" in China. She quit her job in 1986, lived in the US from 1990-1991, and returned to Chengdu in 1992. She opened a bar called White Night in 1998. Among her best known works are "Woman," "Call It Everything," and "Jing'an Village."

张晓红，荷兰莱顿大学文学博士，现任深圳大学外国语学院比较文学副教授。已出版英文著作《The Invention of a Discourse》（2004），中文合著《苍山夜话》（2006）以及中文专著《互文视野中的女性诗歌》（2008）。在《加拿大比较文学评论》、《欧洲研究》等国内外文学刊物上发表论文 30 多篇并出版五部译著。

Zhang Xiaohong is associate professor in comparative literature and chair of Literature Department at Shenzhen University, People's Republic of China. She obtained her PhD in 2004 from Leiden University, the Netherlands. She has published three books: *The Invention of a Discourse* (2004), *Night Talks at the Foot of Cang Mountain* (*Cangshan yehua*, 2006) and *Women's Poetry from an Intertextual Perspective* (*Huwen shiye zhong de nüxing shige*, 2008).

She has published in *Canadian Review of Comparative Literature, European Review* and other distinguished international and Chinese journals, as well as five books translated from English.

宇丽娟，1982年10月29日生于云南凤庆。曾在云南大学学习英语和美学，2007年获哲学硕士学位。现在德国弗莱堡精神病治疗中心工作。

Zi Lijuan was born in Fengqing, Yunnan Province, China on October 29, 1982. She studied English and aesthetics at Yunnan University. She was granted a Master's Degree in Philosophy in 2007. She works at the Center of Psychiatry Emmendingen in Freiburg, Germany.

Index of Poems by Author

Wendy Barker 温迪·巴克·Single Cirrus 17; 孤云 17; Thunder 23; 雷鸣 23; Condensation Nuclei 102; 致密的核 103; Full Moon, Cirrocumulus, Light Breeze, and Iridescence 208; 满月、卷积云、清风和虹彩 209; Near-Earth Object 212; 临近地球的物体 213

Alan Berecka 艾伦·巴拉克·The Last Laugh 154; 最后一笑 155; Winter Wedding 224; 冬日婚礼 225

Jerry Bradley 杰里·布拉得雷·La Vida Nada 20; 虚空的生活 21; Afterward 66; 之后 67; A Single Sheep, One Cow 150; 一只绵羊，一头牛 151; Cleaving a Valentine 222; 情人节的断肠人 223

Nathan Brown 内森·布朗·For Some Reason 36; 因故 37; Burn 72; 燃烧 73; A Note of Thanks 76; 道谢便条 76; Renovations at the Santuario de Guadalupe 164; 翻新德瓜达卢佩圣殿 165

Jerry Craven 杰里·克莱文·Beyond the Entropy of Gophers 82; 地鼠的混沌之外 83; Before the Coming of the Crow 96; 乌鸦来临之前 97; Spring in Palo Duro Canyon 99; 帕罗杜若峡谷的春天 99; Midsummer Farewell 144; 仲夏之别 145

Sherry Craven 雪莉·克莱文·Windmills 106; 风车 107; Holy is a fragile thing... 114; 神圣是个纤弱的东西…… 115; Kite Flying 220; 断线的风筝 221

Patricia Goodrich 帕特丽夏·古德里奇·Drink Water 122; 饮水 123; Our Lady 160; 我们的圣女 160; Low Pressure 200; 低压 200

Kenneth Hada 肯尼斯·哈达·Grace Strokes 126; 优雅地划桨 127; That Which Clings 180; 那紧缠的 181

海男 Hai Nan·故事和鸟群，海男 28; stories and flocks of birds 28; 内衣

的谜诀 44; the riddle of lingerie 44; 面对镜子 45; face to face with the mirror 45; 贪婪 75; greed 75; 鸟群的声音 86; the flock's voice 86; 蝴蝶是怎样变成标本的 87; how a butterfly becomes a specimen 87; 玻璃的味道 95; the flavor of glass 95; 漂亮的奴隶 98; a pretty slave 98; 私秘中的露台 124; private balcony 124; 当天晚上 201; that night 201; 虚构的玫瑰 210; illusive roses 210; 干燥的南部山冈 211; dry, dry southern hills 211; 到底是谁出卖了我 217; who sold me out in the end? 217

Alysa Hayes 艾莉莎 · 海斯 · Gift 140; 礼物 141; Blue in the Middle of a Corn Field 148; 玉米地里的忧伤 148; Pastoral 176; 田园 177; a section from "Games" 230; 节选自《游戏》231

何小竹 He Xiaozhu · 读李后主词仿十四行诗 46; in the manner of a sonnet, on reading lyric verse by Li Yu, last monarch of Southern Tang 47; 梦见苹果和鱼的安 64; dream of apples and fish 65; 送一颗炮弹到喜玛拉雅山顶 94; shoot a bomb to the top of the Himalayas 94; 不是一头牛，而是一群牛 149; not one head of cattle, but a herd of cattle 149; 色达草原 202; Seda Prairie 203

James Hoggard 詹姆斯 · 霍葛德 · This Alien Place Called Home 42; 这个叫作家的鬼地方 43; Anniversary Trip 54; 周年纪念的旅程 55; Red-tailed Hawk 85; 红尾鹰 85

黄芳 Huang Fang · 我就将爱上五月 118; I will fall in love with May 118; 平安夜 158; Christmas Eve 159; 仿佛这忧伤 218; as if this sadness, were real 219

吉木狼格 Jimu Langge · 这一天 112; this day 113; 阿根廷蚂蚁 142; Argentine ants 143; 押韵是有瘾的 146; rhyming is addictive 147; 爱情和马 178; love and horse 179; 西昌的月亮 207; Xichang moon 207

李南 Li Nan · 我去过许多地方⋯⋯ 18; I have been in many places⋯⋯ 19; 时光 24; time 25; 故乡，李南 77; hometown 77; 打开诗篇 104; break open psalms 105; 遥寄江南 120; mail from the southern reaches of the

Yangtze 121; 在广阔的世界上 125; in the wide world 125; 疼 128; it hurts 129; 瓦蓝瓦蓝的天空 196; pastel blue sky 197

李森 Li Sen · 动荡不安的树叶 22; turbulent leaves 22; 坟墓 74; grave 74; 声音和羽毛 84; sounds and feathers 84; 鸟禽畜牲都好歌 88; song for the good birds and beasts 89; 昆明的玫瑰 152; Kunming roses 153; 庭院 167; courtyard 167; 红土高原 198; red earth plateau 199

刘春 Liu Chun · 梦见一个死于车祸的朋友 58; dream of a friend who died in a car accident 59; 我写下的都是卑微的事物 108; all I write about are insignificant things 109; 卡夫卡 170; Kafka 171

Natasha Marin 娜塔莎·马林 · The Family Secret 48; 家庭秘密 49; a nightingale risks 110; 夜莺冒险 111; Yu's Wife 226; 禹的妻子 227

David Meischen 大卫·麦森 · Dry Spell 78; 干旱期 79; Mirage 130; 海市蜃楼 131; Onion Creek, Fall 166; 洋葱河，秋天 166; Nobody's Sugar Daddy Now 228; 现在落单的甜爹 229

冉仲景 Ran Zhongjing · 等待 132; waiting 132; 毛妹，店 162; Mao Mei, shop 163; 夸耀 182; exaltation 183; 摆手舞曲：春天 192; hand-waving dance: spring 192; 债务 194; debt 195; 减法 216; subtraction 216

Aaron Rudolph 阿龙·鲁道夫 · December 70; 十二月 71; The Acuña Brothers Look North, 1952 134; 阿库纳弟兄看北方，1952 年 135; Downtown Albuquerque 172; 爱伯克奇市中心 173

Steven Schroeder 史蒂文·施罗德 · Quixote 30; 堂吉诃德 31; train in the desert at night 168; 行驶在沙漠夜色中的列车 169; prevailing time 193; 盛行的时令 193; Woody Guthrie Memorial Highway 204; 树木茂密的高斯里公路 205; almost human 206; 近乎人类 206

唐丹鸿 Tang Danhong · 他们骂弯了清晨一米 52; they shout abuses till early morning bends one meter 53; 躺在三天宽的歌喉上 100; lie down on a voice singing three days wide 101; 花儿 119; bloom 119; 机关枪新娘 174; machine gun bride 175

Larry Thomas 赖里 · 托马斯 · Mockingbird 92; 水蒲苇莺 93; Blue Norther 186; 蓝色北风 187; Harvest Moon 214; 满月 215; Dust Storm 232; 沙尘暴 233

Scott Wiggerman 司各特 · 威格曼 · In Celebration of Gray 26; 庆祝灰色 27; September 60; 九月 60; October Revival in Texas 62; 德克萨斯十月的 复活 63; West of Fort Worth 184; 沃斯城堡以西 185

杨晓芸 Yang Xiaoyun · 甘蔗林 29; sugarcane forest 29; 回故里 61; going back to the old neighborhood 61; 那些花 133; those flowers 133; 桃花 161; peach blossom 161

瞿永明 Zhai Yongming · 身体 32; bodies 33; 在古代 38; in ancient time 39; 五十年代的语言 136; 1950s language 137; 重阳登高 188; mountain climbing on double nine day 189